The Spirituality of Kintsugi
Hiroki Kiyokawa

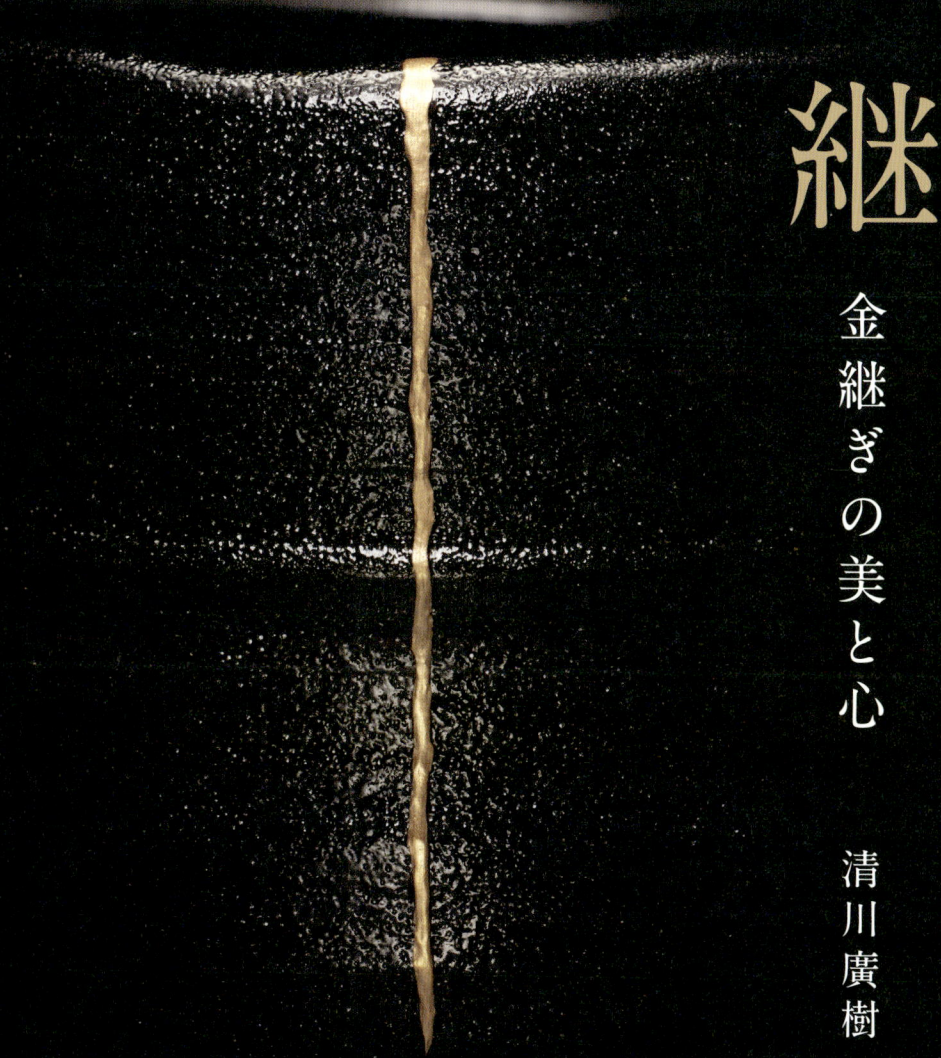

継 つなぐ

金継ぎの美と心

清川廣樹

淡交社 | TANKOSHA

目次

はじめに　　土にかえる ·· 6

一章　　金継ぎと漆芸の世界　その歴史と技法 ······················ 10

　　　　金継ぎとは　　　　　　　　　　　　12
　　　　金継ぎ修復の工程　　　　　　　　　14
　　　　漆のゆりかご・室について　　　　　17
　　　　漆について　　　　　　　　　　　　18
　　　　今に伝わる繕いの名品　　　　　　　28

　　　　コラム 1 ── 漆にまつわる昔話・うるし兄弟と龍の淵 ················ 32

二章　　職人の世界 ··· 36

　　　　生活文化と職人　　　　　　　　　　38
　　　　漆文化のはじまり、大陸文化との出会い　40
　　　　徒弟制度と御礼奉公　　　　　　　　42
　　　　職人文化の衰退への危機感　　　　　44
　　　　修復職人としての心構え　　　　　　48
　　　　千年の釘にいどむ　　　　　　　　　52
　　　　金箔を貼る　　　　　　　　　　　　54

　　　　コラム 2 ── 高野教会のマリア像 ·· 58

三章　　繕うこと、その精神性と文化、世界とのつながり ············ 64

　　　　私の考える茶道と繕い ── 利休と織部に思う　66
　　　　海外に渡った日本の漆芸　　　　　　72

海外からみた繕い　　　　　　　　　　　　　75
　　　　　国連事務総長のスピーチ　　　　　　　77
　　　　　出会い 1　新しい景色、新しい一日　　80
　　　　　出会い 2　想いをつなぐ　　　　　　　82
　　　　　出会い 3　先端と伝統の融合　　　　　85
　　　　　出会い 4　アンブレイカブル Unbreakable　86
　　　琵琶法師との出会い　　　　　　　　　　　88
　　　お茶碗を直す　少年から頼まれた繕い　　　94

　　　コラム 3 ── 清川先生と歩く ｜ 渡邉浩之　漆芸舎スタッフ　　　　96

四章　**私の金継ぎ修復の工程**　　　　　　　　　　　　　　　　102

　　　修復のデザイン　　　　　　　　　　　　　104
　　　金継ぎに使用する道具　　　　　　　　　　110
　　　漆との付き合い方　　　　　　　　　　　　114
　　　「かすがい」による接着強化　　　　　　　122
　　　金継ぎ修復の工程　　　　　　　　　　　　124
　　　　　接着 → 錆付け → 研ぎ → 下地塗り → 装飾 → 粉固め

清川廣樹　金継ぎ修復作品　　　　　　　　　　　　　　　145

特別対談　　　　　　　　　　　　　　　　　　　　　　　　156
人を繋ぐ名もなき茶碗
　　　瀬川日照　本法寺 貫首　×　清川廣樹　修復師

おわりに　　　　　　　　　　　　　　　　　　　　　　　　168
謝辞　　　　　　　　　　　　　　　　　　　　　　　　　　172
プロフィール　　　　　　　　　　　　　　　　　　　　　　174

CONTENTES

Introduction	Return to the Earth	6

Chapter 1 — The World of Kintsugi and Lacquerware History and Techniques 10

What is Kintsugi?	12
The kintsugi process	14
Lacquer's Cradle, the Muro	17
About Urushi	18
A masterpiece among restored vessels handed down from the past	28

Column 1 — An old story about lacquer
The Lacquer Brothers and the Dragon's Pool 32

Chapter 2 — The Craftsman's World 36

The Roots of Kintsugi in Everyday Life	38
The Beginning of Urushi Culture, Encounters with Continental Culture	40
The Apprentice System and Service Work	42
A Sense of Crisis Over the Decline of Craftsman Culture	44
A Restorer's Attitude	48
Meeting the Challenge of a Thousand-year-old Nail	52
Gold Leafing	54

Column 2 — The Statue of Mary at Takano Church 58

Chapter 3 — The World around Kintsugi Restoration 64

My Thoughts on Chado and Restoration: Rikyu and Oribe	66
Japanese Lacquerware that has Gone Overseas	72

	Kintsugi as Seen from Overseas	75
	Speech by the Secretary-General of the United Nations	77
	Encounter 1 A New View and a New Start	80
	Encounter 2 Passing Memories on to the Future	82
	Encounter 3 Fusion of Advanced Technology and Traditional Techniques	85
	Encounter 4 Unbreakable	86
	A Request for Biwa Restoration from Master Musician Kakuyu Sekikawa	88
	Restoring a Rice Bowl A boy's request	94
	Column 3 — Walking with Mr. Kiyokawa By Hiroshi Watanabe, senior manager of Kiyokawa Lacquerware Art	96

Chapter 4   My Kintsugi Restoration Process — 102

Design	104
Tools	110
How to get along with lacquer	114
Strengthening of adhesion with kasugai	122
The Steps in the Kintsugi Restoration Process	124
Adhesion → Applying sabi-urushi → Sanding down → Undercoating → Decoration → Powder cementing	

Works Restored with Kintsugi by Hiroki Kiyokawa — 145

A conversation between
Connecting through the Enigma of a Kitchen Bowl — 156

    Nissho Segawa abbot of Honpoji Temple

    Hiroki Kiyokawa traditional restorer

Afterword	168
Acknowledgments	172
Profile	174

Note

In this book, the names of Japanese historical figures are written surname first, in keeping with Japan's traditional name order.

はじめに ｜ Introduction

土にかえる
Return to the Earth

地球上の動植物は時が経てば全て土にかえります。当たり前のことですが、私たちは普段自分が土にかえることを意識することはありません。

　私は「金継ぎ修復」や「漆芸修復」の際、全てを土にかえすことを前提に、自然素材のみを使って仕事をします。昨今の化学素材を使う近代工法は、利便性に長ける反面、土にかえることはなく、その耐久性についてはまだまだ歴史が浅いです。なおかつ、化学素材は器を傷めてしまい、結果的にその寿命を早めてしまいます。

　一方、美術館などには自然素材で修復した器が1世紀を超えて残っていますが、それは自然素材の耐久性を示す確かな証拠です。

　私は金継ぎを行っている時、自分と自然が共生しているように感じます。金継ぎを含む「漆芸」は漆の木の樹液を採取して行う工法であり、木の命である樹液は、いわば私たちの血液と同じです。自然への敬意を払って修復を行う時、私も自然界の一部であり、やがてこの身は土にかえり、新たな命の一部になることを想います。漆は硬化し、器に同化することで己の存在を残しますが、これには自然に順応して生きようとする日本人の死生観、無常観に通ずるものがあると思います。

　金継ぎの文化は、茶の湯の文化の中で生まれ、育まれてきました。室町時代の茶人たちは茶碗の損なわれた部分を継ぐこと

All living things in our world, all the plants and animals surrounding us, must return to the earth when their time comes. This return is natural, indeed inevitable, but generally we do not think of it much.

When I do kintsugi, I use only natural materials, and consciously work on the premise that everything should be returned to the earth. Though it is convenient to use chemical materials for restoration, but they do not return to the earth, and their durability is still in its infancy. Chemical materials may in fact damage the original vessel. They do not return readily to the soil, and because they have been employed only recently, their durability is untested. On the other hand, vessels restored with natural materials have survived for hundreds of years, solid evidence of their durability.

When I work with kintsugi, I feel harmony with nature. The multiform arts of lacquerware, including kintsugi, employ processes using the sap of the lacquer tree, the very lifeblood of the tree. When I consider this fact, I feel profound gratitude and respect for nature. When I touch the work with my hands, I feel acutely that I too am part of the natural world. Like all elements of that world, my body too will eventually return to the earth, becoming part of a new life. Lacquer hardens and assimilates into the vessel, leaving behind its previous existence and transforming into something new. The contours of this process conform with the traditional Japanese view of life and impermanence, which encourages appreciation of this very moment, and seeing the panorama of inevitable change as natural, and indeed beautiful, adaptations to the profound endless cycles of life and rebirth.

The culture of kintsugi was born and nurtured in chado, the "way of tea." In their careful and attentive repair of damaged matcha bowls, the

で、「壊れ」の中に新たな美を見出し、愛でてきました。その過程で金による装飾が生まれたのです。器に金継ぎ修復を行うことで、割れ欠けを生かした新しい景色が生まれます。

　私は「かたちあるものはいつか壊れる宿命にある」と考え、「壊れること」を悪いこととは捉えません。昨今、壊れた器に自らの人生を投影し、傷ついたことや失敗したことを否定せず受け入れ、「未来をもう一度つくりなおす」という考えが、金継ぎ修復に重ねられています。世界的にも金継ぎ文化が注目され、大量生産、大量消費が加速する時代の中でモノを大切にする精神の大事さ、学校での情操教育や国際的紛争解決の例えにも、その精神性が引用されるようになっています。これは、2015年9月の国連サミットで、加盟国の全会一致で採択されたSDGs（持続可能な開発目標）の普遍性にも共通するものがあると思っています。

　漆も、器も、私自身も、「すべてが土にかえるからこそ、この世に在るうちに、割れ欠けから生まれる美を楽しみたい」。私はそのような思いで今日も金継ぎと向き合っています。私の手仕事に自然の命が宿ることを願い、器が穏やかに土にかえるように修復を行っています。

tea masters of the Muromachi period (1336–1573) discovered, and exulted in, a new beauty of "brokenness." They grew to see in the cracks and fissures of broken bowls the minute and concrete manifestation of the great processes of life and death, and their appreciation lead to the application of gold to accent the broken parts. The techniques of kintsugi restoration give birth not only to a repaired vessel, but to a new view of the vessel by accenting, indeed celebrating, its broken parts.

In line with this view, I do not consider breakage to be a negative thing. I firmly believe that all things that have form are destined to break someday. Moreover, a breakage creates the possibility of reconstructing the future. Like the tea masters of the Muromachi period, gazing with joy at a once-broken tea bowl repaired with gold, the kintsugi view encourages us to interpret the 'breakages' in our life as new starting points, to see damage, disappointment, and failure as profound natural phenomena worthy of appreciation.

Kintsugi culture is attracting attention worldwide. In this age of mass production and mass consumption, the importance of cherishing things and the spirituality of kintsugi provide excellent models in emotional education at schools and as analogies for international conflict resolution. The kintsugi approach approximates the fundamental philosophy of SDGs (Sustainable Development Goals).

Because everything returns to the earth, including lacquer, vessels, and me, I want to enjoy the beauty created by the cracks of age and mishaps of life. I hope that my handiwork emerges with the life of nature fully expressed. I restore vessels so that they may return to the earth peacefully.

一章 | Chapter 1

金継ぎと漆芸の世界
その歴史と技法

The World of Kintsugi and Lacquerware
History and Techniques

金継ぎと漆芸の世界 | The World of Kintsugi and Lacquerware

金継ぎとは
What is Kintsugi?

「金継ぎ」とは、陶器などの修復技法のことを指します。金継ぎ修復は、陶器に限らず、磁器やガラス器、漆器など多岐にわたります。

最近、私は合成樹脂やプラスチック製品の割れ欠けの修復にも挑戦しました。私が習得した江戸時代から伝わる職人技法が、現代製品の修復に応用できるか試してみたかったのです。試行錯誤しましたが、持ち主の方のご期待に沿えるような修復ができたと思います。

金継ぎは漆で継いだ部分の装飾を指し、名前の通り金で行いますが、方法は実にいろいろで、器によっては金を使わない方が良い場合もあります。その他に、青、黒、緑などの色漆による仕上げ、白金、銀、錫等による仕上げ、螺鈿（貝殻）、卵殻を用いた仕上げなど、装飾は多岐にわたります。また金にも、柔らかな輝きを持つものもあれば、金属的な輝きを持つものもあります。

継ぎ方にも「鉛継ぎ」「ガラス継ぎ」「溜継ぎ」「共直し」など様々な技法があり、昔は自分の得意な技法に特化した職人もいました。現代においては、これら多様な装飾方法、継ぎ方を総称して「金継ぎ」といっています。

Kintsugi refers to a genre of traditional techniques for restoring ceramics and other vessels. Not only pottery, but also porcelain, glassware and lacquerware can be restored using its methods. Recently, I have even tried my hand at repairing cracks and chips in synthetic resin and plastic products. I was curious to see if traditional artisanal techniques in use since the Edo period could be applied to the restoration of modern products. It took a lot of trial and error, but I believe I was able to restore the product to meet the owner's expectations.

As the name suggests, gold is used to decorate in kintsugi, but in fact, many natural materials are used in its techniques. Sometimes it is better not to use gold for restoration. A wide range of decorations exist, and depending on the vessel the process may involve finishing with blue, black, green or other colored lacquer, with platinum, silver, tin, or other metals, or with mother-of-pearl inlays and eggshells. Some gold has a soft glow, while other types have a more metallic shine. In the past, craftsmen formulated and then specialized in their own signature techniques. In modern times, the term "kintsugi" is used as an umbrella term to refer to all of these various historical decorative methods and techniques.

金継ぎとは
金継ぎ修復の工程

基本となる修復工程は次の通りです。

1. 接着 　　割れ欠けした箇所を、生漆と米粉を混ぜてつくった「のり漆」で合わせる。

2. 錆付け　　生漆と山の土（砥の粉）を混ぜてつくった「錆漆」を「のり漆」の上に盛る。

3. 研ぎ　　「錆漆」を鑢で研いで、想いのかたちを形成する。

4. 下地塗り　形成した「錆漆」に「黒漆」を中塗り、上塗りの2回塗る。

5. 装飾　　黒漆の上に弁柄漆を塗り、それが完全に乾く前に金粉を蒔く。

6. 粉固め　金粉が完全に定着したら、生漆でコーティングする。

　破損状況にもよりますが、修復作業は6〜10工程ほどで行われ、漆の乾燥日数を含めると完成まで2〜3か月を要します。割れ部分の接着は「のり漆」が基本ですが、さらに強度を高める場合は、表具師が用いる伝統技法を接着に応用したり、竹でつくった「かすがい」を施したりします。欠け部分が失われている場合は、小さな欠けであれば「錆漆」で盛りつけ形成します。大きな欠けであれば、昔から伝わる漆と繊維を組み合わせる「乾漆」の技法を応用して欠け部分を再現して修復します。

page 124 — Chapter 4
金継ぎ修復の工程
The kintsugi process

What is Kintsugi?

The kintsugi process

The basic steps in the process are as follows:

1. The cracked and chipped parts are first glued together with nori-urushi, "glue lacquer," which is a mixture of raw urushi and rice powder. This material begins the restoration process, but due to evaporation of the water content of the rice powder, this glue is not stable on its own.

2. The nori-urushi is then covered with sabi-urushi, which is a mixture of raw urushi and powdered clay, called tonoko. The tonoko provides stability and the resultant putty-like substance dries to a hard finish.

3. After drying, the sabi-urushi is sanded to form the desired shape.

4. Black urushi is then applied on the now sanded and shaped sabi-urushi at least two times (middle coat, top coat). This is the waterproofing process.

5. After the top coat is finished, bengara-urushi, which is a mixture of raw urushi and red iron oxide pigment, is applied. Before the drying process of the bengara-urushi is completed, when just a thin film is formed on the surface, high-purity gold powder is sown onto the surface.

6. Once the bengara-urushi is dry and the gold powder is completely fixed, the surface is coated with final coat of raw urushi. This process is called 'powder cementing'.

Depending on the damage to the vessel, the restoration process involves repetitions of the above to a total of 6 to 10 steps. Including the drying time of the lacquer, which can be longer or shorter depending on the season and the ambient humidity, the entire process takes 2 to 3 months to complete. Generally, the cracks are repaired with glue lacquer, but to increase the strength of the mend, traditional techniques employed by scroll mounters, or kasugai clamps made of bamboo or metal might be applied. If there is a small missing part, the space is filled in with sabi-urushi. For larger missing parts, the traditional technique for creating kanshitsu "dry lacquer" articles is used to recreate the part. In this technique, nori-urushi is mixed with fibrous material to increase its strength, molded into shape, and then covered with sabi-urushi.

金継ぎ修復の工程 | The kintsugi process

漆のゆりかご・室について
Lacquer's Cradle, the Muro

接着された器は各工程が終わるごとに室の中に置かれ、漆の乾燥と硬化を待ちます。室は樹液である漆が眠りにつき、ゆっくり乾燥して硬化し、器の一部となるのを迎えるための、漆の「ゆりかご」のような場所です。

私たちは乾燥というと、水分が空気中に蒸発することをイメージしますが、漆は正反対で、空気中の水分を吸収して乾いていきます。室は密閉された木棚で、杉でつくられています。日本の固有種である杉は優れた調湿作用と調温作用を持っており、古くは奈良・東大寺の正倉院宝庫でも使われていることが分かっています。室の中は湿度75%前後、温度20〜25度前後に保たれています。湿度が高いのは、漆が自然素材であり、呼吸をしているためです。人間が快適に過ごせる湿度は50%といわれています。漆も人間同様、乾燥と硬化のためには適正な湿度が必要です。

また、漆は乾くのに時間がかかる特徴があります。ゆっくり乾くことで、合成塗料とは比べ物にならない堅牢さ、耐水性、防腐性を得ることができます。私たち職人は、漆がベストの状態で器に同化するよう室の調湿、調温管理をしなければなりません。漆の乾燥日数は修復期間中の天候や湿度に大きく左右されます。

At the end of each process, the glued vessels are placed in a chamber called "muro," for the lacquer to dry and harden. The muro is like a cradle for the lacquer, where the lacquer sap 'goes to sleep' and slowly dries, hardening to become part of the vessel. When we think of drying, we think of moisture evaporating into the air. However, lacquer is the exact opposite: it absorbs moisture from the air and dries. The muro is an enclosed wooden cabinet made of sugi, or Japanese cedar. This indigenous tree species has excellent moisture and temperature regulating properties, and is known to have been used in the Shosoin treasure house in Nara, which dates to the mid 8th century. Inside the muro, the temperature is kept at around 20-25 degrees Celsius and the humidity at around 75%. The high humidity is due to the fact that lacquer is a natural material and it breathes. It is said that the humidity at which humans can live comfortably is 50%. Lacquer needs an appropriate amount of humidity for drying and hardening, and lacquer takes a long time to dry. By drying slowly, the lacquer provides robustness, water resistance, and antiseptic properties that are remarkably superior to synthetic paints. Craftsmen do their best to control the temperature and humidity of the muro so that the applied lacquer can be assimilated into the vessel in the best condition. Inevitably the drying time of the lacquer depends largely on the weather and humidity during the restoration period.

金継ぎと漆芸の世界
漆について

　漆とは、漆の木の幹から採取した樹液を精製したものです。樹液の主成分であるウルシオールが酸化し固まることで、強い耐久性、耐水性、断熱性、防腐性を持ちます。現代の化学塗料より強靭で優れた性質を持ち、金継ぎやその他の伝統工芸などで接着剤として利用されてきました。金継ぎを語る上で漆の歴史と特性は外すことはできません。

漆の歴史

　日本人と漆の関わりには長い歴史があります。
　複数の縄文時代の遺跡からは、漆を施した装飾品が出土しています。1975年、福井県若狭町の鳥浜貝塚からは約6100年前の赤色の漆の櫛が出土しました。この櫛は、「漆文化のシンボル」ともいわれています。また、同遺跡からは約1万2600年前のものとされる世界最古の漆の木片も発見されました。漆はもともと中国大陸から伝わったとされていましたが、この木片発見により、漆は日本発祥との説も浮上しています。
　さらに、北海道函館市・垣ノ島遺跡からは、約9000年前の漆塗りの衣服が見つかりました。この他にも全国の遺跡から朱塗りの埴輪や木鉢など、漆塗りを施した多くの生活道具が見つかっています。縄文時代にはすでに赤い漆と黒い漆が存在しており、土器を装飾する手法として松葉を漆に押し当てて模様を施すことも行われていました。
　弥生時代に入り定住生活が進むと、農耕具や漁具など多岐にわたって漆が活用され始めます。
　飛鳥・奈良・平安時代には、仏教の伝来とともに寺院や仏像、仏具などに多くの漆が使われるようになり、漆の芸術的な役割が増していきます。奈良時代の代表的な仏像である興福寺・阿修羅像（奈良県奈良市）では、仏像の原型を粘土でつくり麻布を被せ、漆で麻布を固めて仕上げる「脱活乾漆」という技法が使われています。平安時代には漆塗りの上に金箔を施した中尊寺金色堂（岩手県西磐井郡平泉町）が建立されています。全体に蒔絵や螺鈿の装飾が施されたお堂は、漆芸の頂点を極める建造物として今も輝きを放っています。
　鎌倉・室町時代になると、日常的に使う食器や武士の刀などにも漆が用いられ、漆器づくりが産業として盛んになります。

The World of Kintsugi and Lacquerware

About Urushi

Urushi, natural lacquer, is made of the purified sap from the trunk of the urushi tree (*Toxicodendron vernicifluum*). Urushiol, the main component of the sap, oxidizes and hardens, making it highly durable, water-resistant, insulating, and antiseptic. Tougher and more durable than modern chemical paints, urushi has been used historically as an adhesive in kintsugi and other traditional crafts. The history and characteristics of urushi cannot be ignored in a discussion of kintsugi.

The history of urushi

The relationship between the Japanese people and urushi has a long history.

In 1975, a 6,100-year-old comb lacquered in red urushi was unearthed from the Torihama shell mound in Wakasa Town, Fukui Prefecture. This comb is said to be a symbol of urushi culture. The world's oldest piece of urushi wood, believed to be about 12,600 years old, was also discovered at the same site.

Urushi was originally thought to have been introduced from the Chinese continent, but the discovery of this piece of wood has raised the theory that it originated in Japan. At the Kakinoshima site in Hakodate, Hokkaido, urushi-lacquered clothing from the early Jomon period (about 9,000 years ago) was found. Vermilion urushi-lacquered haniwa (clay figurines) and urushi-lacquered household items such as wooden bowls have also been found at archaeological sites throughout Japan.

In the Jomon period, red urushi and black urushi already existed, and the technique of decorating earthenware with patterns by pressing pine needles against the urushi was also used. In the Yayoi period, when people began to settle down, urushi was used for a wide range of purposes, including in the production of farming and fishing tools. In the Asuka, Nara, and Heian periods, with the introduction of Buddhism, urushi was used in many temples, Buddhist statues, and Buddhist implements, and it's artistic role increased.

The Asura statue at Kofukuji Temple, one of the most famous Buddhist statues from the Nara period, uses a technique called "hollow dry lacquer" in which an original clay statue is covered with hemp, and finished by hardening the hemp with urushi. In the Heian period (794–1185), the Konjikido Hall at Chusonji Temple (Hiraizumi-cho, Nishiwani-gun, Iwate Prefecture) was built with gold leaf applied over urushi. The entire hall was decorated with meki-e and mother-of-pearl, and it still shines today as a structure representing the pinnacle of urushi art.

In the Kamakura and Muromachi periods (1192–1333;1336–1573), urushi was used for daily tableware and sword accountrements for samurai, and urushi lacquerware became a thriving industry.

In the Edo period (1603–1868), lacquerware was produced as a regional specialty throughout Japan, including Wajima lacquerware of Ishikawa Prefecture, Aizu lacquerware of Fukushima Prefecture, and Tsugaru lacquerware

江戸時代に入ると、全国で地域の特産品として、石川県の輪島塗、福島県の会津塗、青森県の津軽塗などの漆器が生産されていきました。この頃、印籠を装飾品として持つことが流行り、様々な技法が用いられた漆の印籠が制作されています。開国により海外との貿易が盛んになると、繊細な日本の漆器は海外で人気が出て、日本の漆芸が「JAPAN（ジャパン）」と呼ばれるようになりました。

　明治・大正・昭和時代前半は、近代化や戦争により高価な漆器の需要が減退しますが、戦後、高度経済成長が始まると漆器の需要は再び高まりました。

　もともと、漆は庶民の生活の近くにあったものでした。昔は各村の畑のそばに漆の木があり、村の人たちは欠けた器の修繕や川沿いの堤防の杭に漆塗りをしていたそうです。畑近くの漆の木は養分が良いためか、木肌が柔らかく採取できる漆の量も多かったといわれています。しかし、漆の木があると作付けがしにくいことから、徐々に漆は村の外で栽培されるようになります。

　現在、国内で流通している漆の約97%が中国産です。日本産としては、岩手県二戸市の浄法寺地区が国内生産量の約70%を占めています。浄法寺地区には約21万本の漆の木があり、約30人の職人が樹液採取のため働いています。以前は300人以上の職人がいましたが、漆器の需要が減るのに伴い減少しています。

of Aomori Prefecture. At that time, it became fashionable to carry on one's person a beautifully decorated portable lacquerware medicine case called inro, and various techniques were used to produce them.

With the opening of the country to foreign trade, delicate Japanese lacquerware became popular overseas, where it came to be known as "Japan." In the Meiji, Taisho, and early Showa periods (a time span roughly from the 1870s to 1950s), demand for expensive lacquerware declined due to modernization and war, but with the start of rapid economic growth after World War II, demand for lacquerware increased again.

Urushi has always been a part of the lives of ordinary people. In the old days, when urushi trees grew near the fields of each village, villagers used to use the sap to repair chipped vessels and to lacquer the river embankment piles. It is said that the urushi trees near the fields had softer bark and provided generous amounts of sap, perhaps due to better nutrients. However, since those trees made it difficult to plant the fields, urushi tree husbandry gradually moved outside the village.

Currently, about 97% of the urushi distributed in Japan comes from China. In Japan, the Joboji district in Ninohe City, Iwate Prefecture, produces about 70% of the domestic production. There are about 210,000 urushi trees in Joboji, and about 30 specialits work there to collect the sap. There used to be more than 300 skilled workers, but the number has decreased as the demand for lacquerware decreases.

漆について | About Urushi

漆の採取
Collecting the sap of the urushi tree

　漆の樹液を採取することを「漆を搔く」といいます。「搔く」とは、漆の木の表皮を剥ぎ、幹に薄く傷をつけ、沁みだしてくる乳白色の樹液をダカッポという専用の手桶に素早く汲む作業のことです。漆の樹液は木の表層のすぐ下のわずかな隙間に流れているので、幹に深く傷をつけると樹液は採れず、木の寿命も短くなってしまいます。漆搔きの職人（搔子）は専用の鎌を使い、長年の経験で絶妙な深さの切り込みを木の幹に入れていきます。

　そうして採取し、濾過したものを「生漆」と呼びます。生漆に「ナヤシ（搔き混ぜて成分を均等にする作業）」や、「クロメ（過熱して水分を飛ばす作業）」などの精製作業を行うと、漆は半透明の飴色になり、これを「透き漆」と呼びます。透き漆に鉄分を混ぜると黒漆になり、顔料を加えると色漆になります。透き漆に顔料を混ぜても淡い色合いは出せないため、一般的に漆の色は朱色、緑色、黄色、青色など濃くはっきりした色が多いです。白漆と呼ばれる漆は、飴色の透き漆に白の顔料を混ぜるので、完全な白ではなくベージュのような色になります。

Collecting the sap of the urushi tree is called "scraping." The process of scraping involves peeling off the bark of the tree, making thin, shallow scratches on the trunk, and quickly drawing the milky sap into a special bucket called a 'dakappo'. The sap flows in a shallow region just below the surface of the tree, so if the trunk is scratched too deeply, the sap cannot be collected, and the life of the tree is jeopardized. The skilled workers (called 'kakiko') who handle this work use a specialized kind of sickle, and through years of experience, they make cuts of perfect depth in the tree trunk.

The collected and filtered sap is called ki-urushi, or "raw lacquer." When the raw lacquer is subjected to refining processes such as nayashi (stirring to equalize the ingredients) and kurome (intense heating to remove water), it becomes translucent and amber-colored. This is called suki-urushi, "translucent lacquer." When iron is mixed with suki-urushi, it becomes kuro-urushi, "black lacquer," and when pigments are added, it becomes colored lacquer. Pale colors cannot be achieved by adding pigments to suki-urushi, which is why most colored lacquer is of distinct, strong colors such as vermilion, green, yellow, or blue. Lacquer called shiro-urushi, "white lacquer," mixes white pigment with amber-colored suki-urushi, resulting in a beige-like off-white color rather than a perfect white.

漆搔きのようす／画像提供：一般社団法人大子町特産品流通公社
Urushi Scraping / Photo courtesy of General Incorporated Association Daigo Specialty Distribution Company

漆の木が成長して樹液が採れるまで、およそ10〜15年かかるといわれています。1本の木から採れる漆の量はおよそ200mlと少なく、採取を終えた漆の木は死に絶えてしまうため、このことから漆掻き作業は「殺し掻き」といわれています。これは6月から9月にかけて木に傷をつけ、さらに日を空けて11月にも傷をつけ、漆を採取し尽くし、その後は樹幹を伐採する方法です。漆の樹液は幹から沁みだすと、すぐに色が変わり凝固して木の命を守ろうとします。これは人間の血液がかさぶたをつくるのに似ています。掻子は、「漆の一滴は血の一滴」と考え、木の命をいただいていることを忘れず、自然に対する敬意と畏怖をもって仕事に取り組んでいます。漆芸に携わる私たち職人もまた、一滴の漆も無駄にせず、掻子の想いも預かって、漆に向き合わないといけません。

　漆の木は11月後半に伐採され切株になりますが、翌春には切株から新芽がでてきます。また、昔から漆の木は人里近くの土地によく育つといわれています。漆の木はかぶれをもたらす樹液で、人間以外の生物からは身を守り、伐採しても栽培する方法を知っている人間には樹液を採取されることを許している、という伝承があります。このように人間と漆は長い年月、共存してきました。

It takes about 10 to 15 years for the urushi tree to grow and produce sap, and only about 200 milliliters of sap can be extracted from each tree. The trees are scratched from June to September and again in November to collect all the sap, and then the trunks are cut. As the urushi sap oozes out from the trunk, it quickly changes color and coagulates to protect the life of the tree. This is similar to the way human blood forms scabs. The kakiko ("scrapers") consider a drop of urushi sap to be a drop of blood, and never forget that they have received the life of the tree in recompense for their work. In this way the kakiko approach their work with a respect and awe for nature. As lacquerware restorers, we too must consider urushi seriously, not wasting a single drop of it, and keeping the ideals of the kakiko in mind.

Urushi trees are cut down in the latter half of November and become stumps, but new shoots emerge from the stumps in the following spring. It has long been said that urushi trees grow best in areas near human settlements. According to a traditional explanation, the urushi tree protects itself from non-human creatures with its rash-inducing sap, but allows the sap to be collected by people, who know how to care for the tree even after its sap is harvested. In this way, humans and urushi trees have coexisted for many generations.

漆の森
Lacquer-tree grove

漆について | About Urushi

漆の抗菌作用
Antibacterial properties of lacquer

　昔、おせち料理を数日間、漆塗りの重箱の中に入れて保管していましたが、これには理由があります。それは、冷蔵庫やスーパーマーケットがなかった時代の人々が「漆塗りの器に入れた料理は他の器に比べて腐りにくい」ということを知っていたからです。重箱に盛りつけるのは、年の初めの儀式的な趣を感じますが、昔の人は、生活の中で漆の抗菌作用に気づいていました。他にも、水の保存には漆桶を使ったり、カビの生えやすいパンや餅は杉でつくった漆箱に入れたりしています。 漆を塗った花器に生けた花は長持ちするという話もあるようです。漆の抗菌作用については近頃、様々な研究が行われ、実証されています。

In the old times, there was a reason why Osechi (the traditional dishes prepared for the New Year's holiday) was stored in urushi lacquered boxes. It was because in the days before refrigerators and supermarkets, people knew that prepared foods stored in lacquered containers were less likely to spoil than if kept in other kinds of containers. For us modern Japanese, serving New Year's food in lacquered jubako ("stacked boxes") feels mostly ritualistic, a nostalgic acknowledgement of the holiday, but people in the past chose lacquerware for its antibacterial properties. Cooking was not allowed during the three-day period of the New Year, and food stored in the lacquered vessels would keep well throughout the holiday. Lacquered vats have been used for storing water, and lacquered boxes made of cedar protect bread and rice cakes from mold. Flowers arranged in lacquered vases are said to last longer. The antibacterial effect of lacquer has recently been the subject of various studies, and its efficacy proven.

重箱
Japanese lacquered box

写真／Photo | 大道雪代／Yukiyo Daido

金継ぎと漆芸の世界

今に伝わる繕いの名品

　「はじめに」でも申し上げましたが、金継ぎは、室町時代に茶の湯の文化の中で生まれ、育(はぐく)まれてきました。継ぎ目に金、銀、色漆などで装飾を加えて傷痕を「景色」として愉(たの)しみ、傷をありのままの歴史として受け入れ、新しい調和を生み出します。聞いたところでは、金継ぎされた箇所を「川の流れ」に見立てて愉しんだそうです。繕(つくろ)いを通じて芸術的、美的価値を持たせることで、戦国時代の茶人たちはその美しさを追求していきました。ここでは、現存する代表的な金継ぎ修復作品を3点ご紹介します。

The World of Kintsugi and Lacquerware

A masterpiece among restored vessels handed down from the past

As mentioned in the introduction, kintsugi was born and nurtured in the culture of the tea ceremony during the Muromachi period (1336–1573). By decorating the cracks and fissures of broken vessels with gold, silver, and colored lacquer, the tea masters of those days were practicing a worldview. They were training their minds to not merely accept them. The mistakes of the past and the damages of happenstance.

In applying kintsugi to broken vessels, they celebrated the breakage and transformed the vessels. The masters of this worldview enjoyed tracing the "flowing rivers" of the gilded joints, reposing in the afterglow of damaged areas now scintillating with gold and color. The tea masters of the Sengoku period (Warring States period, 1467–1568) pursued beauty in their works by restoring the work's damaged parts. Below are three of the most representative historical examples of kintsugi restoration.

Image: TNM Image Archives

青磁茶碗　銘 馬蝗絆

重要文化財
南宋時代
龍泉窯
東京国立博物館蔵

　日本に伝えられた青磁茶碗の中でも、姿、釉色が特に美しいばかりではなく、その伝来にまつわる逸話によって広く知られている作品です。室町時代に将軍足利義政（在位1449〜73）が所持するところとなりましたが、底にひび割れがあったため、中国に送ってこれに替わる茶碗を求めたところ、当時の中国にはこのような優れた青磁茶碗はすでになく、ひび割れをかすがいで留めて日本に送り返してきました。あたかも大きな蝗のように見える鎹が打たれたことによって、この茶碗の評価は一層高まり、「馬蝗絆」と名づけられました。

Celadon Tea Bowl "Bakohan" (Locust Bond)

Southern Song dynasty (China 1127–1279)
Longquan ware
Tokyo National Museum
Important Cultural Property

Among the celadon tea bowls introduced to Japan, this work is not only particularly beautiful in the color of its glaze and overall appearance, but is also widely known for the anecdotes surrounding its introduction. In the Muromachi period (1336–1573), the shogun Ashikaga Yoshimasa (r.1449–73) owned this bowl, but it developed a crack on the bottom, so he sent it to China for a replacement. As there were no celadon bowls of such quality in China at the time, the crack was fixed with clamps and the bowl sent back to Japan. The clamps, which resembled locusts, further enhanced its reputation, and it was given the name "Locust Bond."

赤楽茶碗「雪峯」
本阿弥光悦作

重要文化財
江戸時代
畠山記念館蔵

　腰から胴にかけて丸く張り、鞠のような円満な姿をしているこの赤楽茶碗は、「光悦七種（こうえつしちしゅ）」のひとつに数えられています。全体はやや厚めで、内側に抱え込むような口縁から、胴、高台にかけて、太くて大きな火割れがあり、金粉漆繕いがなされています。この火割れは赤楽としては高火度で焼成したために窯割れが生じたと考えられており、「雪峯（せっぽう）」の名前は、一方の口縁から胴にかけてなだれるようにかけられた白釉を、山嶺（さんれい）に降り積もる白雪にたとえ、また、火割れを雪解けの渓流（けいりゅう）になぞらえて光悦自ら命銘したといわれています。

Red Raku Tea Bowl
"Seppo" (Snowy Mountaintop)
By Hon'ami Koetsu

Early Edo period (ca. 1603–37)
Hatakeyama Memorial Museum
Important Cultural Property

This Red Raku tea bowl, which curves out around its torso and has a round shape like a ball, is one of the "seven types of Koetsu." It is slightly thicker than the others, and from its mouth rim, which seems to hug into the bowl, there are large, thick firing cracks down to its base, which were mended with lacquer and gold powder. The name "Seppo" is said to have been given by Koetsu himself, who likened the white glaze that surges down from the mouth rim to white snow accumulating on a mountain ridge, and the firing cracks to a snowmelt mountain stream.

大井戸茶碗「須弥」
（別名 十文字井戸）

朝鮮時代
三井記念美術館蔵

　古田織部が用いた「破調の美」の表現方法に、器をあえて壊して継ぎ合わせ、そこに生じる美を愉しむという方法があります。その名品が大きさを縮めるために茶碗を十字に断ち切って漆で再接着した「大井戸茶碗　銘須弥　別名十文字井戸」です。故意に形を歪せた遊び心。一度完成した茶碗を壊して継ぎ、傷にさえ美しさを見いだす破調の美。織部は自ら創造するにとどまらず、既存の器の破壊と再生を行うことで己の美意識を楽しんでいます。

Large Ido Tea Bowl "Shumi" (Sumeru); alt. name, "Jumonji" (Cross)

Joseon dynasty (Korea 1392–1910)
Mitsui Memorial Museum

One of Furuta oribe's methods of expressing "the beauty of broken style" was to deliberately break a vessel and then enjoy the beauty that emerges when it is put back together. The photo shows a tea bowl cut crosswise and re-glued with urushi to reduce its size. The broken style finds beauty in breaking the once-intact vessel and joining its parts together in a new, playful, deliberate recreation. Oribe not only created his own works, but also explored his sense of beauty by deliberately destroying existing vessels and joining them together again.

Column 1 コラム

挿画／Illustration ｜ 山本宗平／Sohei Yamamoto

漆にまつわる昔話 ｜ うるし兄弟と龍の淵

　昔、日向国(現在の宮崎県)の山奥、米良という小さな村に、漆採りの兄弟が住んでいました。兄の名は安佐衛門、弟は十兵衛といいました。二人は朝から晩まで漆の木を探して樹液を採っていましたが、なかなか良い木が見つからず、やせた木から採れた漆は高値では売れないため、いつも貧乏な暮らしをしていました。

　ある日、安佐衛門は新しい漆の木を探しに山奥に入りました。山奥のさらに奥に深い青色の水を湛えた淵があり、その近くには見事な漆の木がありました。安佐衛門は喜び勇んで木に近づこうとしたところ、誤って足を滑らせ、鎌を手から離してしまったのです。鎌はがけを滑って淵の水の中に沈んでしまいました。困った安佐衛門は淵に潜ることに決め、水底に着いて探ってみると手が鎌の柄に触れました。柄を摑んだその時、安佐衛門の手は同時にヌルッとしたものに触れました。水面に顔を出して手を見ると、何とそれは漆でした。しかも、極上

Episode | An old story about lacquer

The Lacquer Brothers and the Dragon's Pool

Once upon a time, in a small village called Mera, deep in the mountains of Hyuga (present-day Miyazaki Prefecture), there lived two brothers who were lacquer harvesters. The elder brother was named Yasuzaemon, and the younger was named Jubei. They worked from morning to night to find lacquer trees and collect the sap, but it was difficult to find good trees. The lacquer available from the thinner trees did not fetch a good price, so they lived in poverty.

One day, the elder brother Yasuzaemon wandered far into the mountains to find a good untapped lacquer tree. In a secluded spot deep in the forest, he came upon a pool of deep blue water, and near it was a magnificent lacquer tree. He was so excited to approach the tree that he accidentally slipped, and his harvester's sickle slipped from his hand. The sickle toppled off the edge of the pool and sank into the water. Immediately, the agitated Yasuzaemon dove into the water, and when he reached out towards the bottom of the pool, his hand touched the sickle handle.

As he grabbed the handle, his hand touched something slippery. He rose to the surface to take a look at his hand, and saw that it was covered in lacquer. He realized it was a very fine lacquer, so he dove down again to check it out. To his amazement that he found that the entire bottom of the pool was covered in pure lacquer. Having discovered the magnificent lacquer pool, Yasuzaemon, in his greedy heart, devised how to keep it all for himself.

The next day, he returned to the secluded pool to scoop up the lacquer. Several days later, he and his younger brother Jubei went to the market at Kuma-Omote (in present day Hitoyoshi City, Kumamoto Prefecture) to sell their lacquer. Yasuzaemon's lacquer fetched a much higher price than did Jubei's. Surprised, the younger

brother asked Yasuzaemon where he had found his lacquer, but the older brother would not reveal the place.

One morning, Jubei, who had watched his brother grow rich by selling the finest quality lacquer, secretly followed him as he left the house. He trailed him all the way to the secluded pool and saw him diving into the deep end to scoop up the lacquer. Jubei later returned to the spot and began to collect lacquer from the pool, without telling his brother.

A few days later, the two again went to market to sell their lacquer. This time, both brothers sold their lacquer at an unprecedentedly high price, which surprised the elder brother. Yasuzaemon suspected Jubei's behavior and secretly followed him on his next outing to collect lacquer, only to find his younger brother diving into the depths of the secret pool to collect it.

Yasuzaemon devised a plan. He bought a wooden dragon at Kuma-Omote with the idea to place it at the bottom of the pool so as to terrify his brother and drive him away from ever again collecting lacquer at the pool. When Yasuzaemon dove into the pool and positioned the wooden dragon, he was taken aback for a moment, as the dragon really looked alive, its golden eyes flickering in the depths. Yasuzaemon thought this apparition would surely scare his brother out

の漆だったので、安佐衛門はもう一度潜って確かめました。水底にあったのは、やっぱり漆でした。見事な漆の淵を発見した安佐衛門は、欲深い心でそれを独り占めにしようとしました。

翌日から安佐衛門は、淵の漆を掬いに出かけました。そして弟の十兵衛と一緒に、球磨表（熊本県人吉市）に売りに出かけたところ、安佐衛門の漆は十兵衛のものよりはるかに高価で買い取られました。驚いた十兵衛は安左衛門に漆の在りかを尋ねましたが、安左衛門は十兵衛に教えることはありませんでした。極上の漆を売って豊かになっていく安左衛門をみた十兵衛は、ある朝、秘かに家を出る安左衛門の後をつけ、彼が淵に潜って漆を掬っているのを見てしまいました。それから十兵衛は、安左衛門に内証で淵の漆を採り始めたのです。

幾日か後、二人は漆を売りに出かけました。今度は二人とも今までにない高値で買い取られたものですから、驚いたのは安佐衛門です。十兵衛の様子に気づいた安左衛門が、今度は漆採りにいく十兵衛の後を内緒でつけてみると、彼が淵に潜って漆を採っているのを見つけました。

安佐衛門は一計を案じ、球磨表から木彫りの龍を買って帰り、それを淵の底に置いて弟を追い出そうと考えました。安左衛門が淵に潜って木彫りの龍を置くと、龍はまるで生きているかのように見えました。安左衛門はこれを見たら十兵衛は怖がって二度と漆を採りに来ることはないだろうと思い、安心して家路につきました。数日後、何も知らない十兵衛が淵に潜ってみると、龍が火を噴き、つめを立てて襲いかかってくるではありませんか。驚いた十兵衛は命からがら逃げ帰ると、安左衛門に龍のことを告げました。

安佐衛門は十兵衛の怯え方を見て、これで漆は全部自分のものになったと、ほくそ笑みました。それからしばらくして、安左衛門が再び淵に潜っていくと、そこにいたのは木彫りの龍ではなく、本物の龍でした。龍に襲われた安佐衛門は二度と水面に上がってくることはありませんでした。

何日かたったある日、淵の底に龍の頭の形の石が沈んでいるのが見られました。

参考文献
「神話と伝承101㊻米良の漆兄弟」より
宮崎県ホームページ

of his wits, and satisfied, he left and went home.

A few days later, when Jubei, unaware and unguarded, dove into the pool as usual to collect the lacquer, he was suddenly attacked by a ferocious dragon spewing fire and raking its claws. Terrified, Jubei ran for his life.

When Yasuzaemon saw the terror in Jubei's eyes as the younger brother tearfully recounted the encounter with the dragon, he laughed quietly to himself, thinking that the lacquer was now all his. However, some time after, when he returned to the pool and dove into its depths, a real dragon attacked him. Destroyed by the dragon, he never resurfaced.

Several days later, a stone the shape of a dragon's head was found gazing up from the bottom of the pool.

二章 ｜ Chapter 2

職人の世界
The Craftsman's World

職人の世界
生活文化と職人

　ここ数年注目されている「金継ぎ」ですが、漆を使って器を継ぐ修復は、昔はどこの家でも一般的に行われていました。村の近くには漆の木があり、そこから採ってきた樹液と米を炊いた鍋にこびりついて残ったごはん粒を混ぜ合わせて、割れたり欠けたりした茶碗やお椀を接着するという修復は、若い人に家業を任せ一線を退いた家長の役目だったといいます。また、村には器修復の職人がいたり、番傘修復の職人がいたり、畳の張替え、ふすまの張替えの職人がいたり、日常生活の修復は多様な職人の分業体制で営まれていました。

　私は30〜40代の頃、日本各地の神社仏閣の修復現場の作業に携わってきました。そんな時、寺の蔵屋敷や縁の下から大昔の壊れた器や漆で修理をした湯呑みや皿がたくさん見つかることがありました。昔は壊れた陶磁器の廃棄場所は敷地内の土の中か縁の下だったのでしょう。そんなところから漆で継いだ器がいくつも出てくることがあります。もちろん金の装飾などは施されておらず器としての役割を日常の調度品として回復させ、再利用しているだけです。

しかしながら、それらは美意識や感性を上乗せする金継ぎのルーツそのものです。

　竹や金属でつくった杭のようなもので器を継ぐ「かすがい」の修復は、漆継ぎの原点ともいうべき技法ですが、昔は茶碗や湯呑みの数が少なかったので、職人が各家庭をまわり、かすがいを入れて修復をしていたようです。私もよくかすがいを使った修復を行いますが、京都の工房には「昔は、こういうお茶碗がいっぱいありました」とかすがいを見て懐かしんでおられる方がたくさんいらっしゃいます。なんの飾り気もない手づくりの修復は、人の心をほのぼのとさせます。よく「子はかすがい」といいますが、夫婦の絆をさらに深める子供の存在を「かすがい」に例えるのは、そのように修復された茶碗で食事をする家族の会話の中から生まれたのかもしれません。

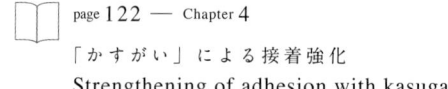

page 122 ── Chapter 4
「かすがい」による接着強化
Strengthening of adhesion with kasugai

The Craftsman's World

The Roots of Kintsugi in Everyday Life

Kintsugi has been attracting a lot of attention in the past few years, but the restoration of vessels using urushi was once a common practice in every household. There was often an urushi tree near the village, and retired patriarchs had the job of repairing cracked and chipped bowls by mixing the sap from the urushi tree with leftover cooked rice. In the village, craftsmen repaired vessels, umbrellas, tatami mats, and fusuma screens (papered sliding doors used to partition off rooms in a Japanese house).

When I was in my 30s and 40s, I was involved in the restoration of temples and shrines all over Japan. We would often live at the temple for the several weeks or months it took to complete the work. I found many broken vessels and lacquer-repaired teacups and plates from long ago in their storehouses or under their buildings. In the old days, probably the place to dispose of broken ceramics was in the ground or in the crawl space beneath the buildings on one's property. In such places, you can find many lacquer-repaired vessels. Of course, they were not decorated with gold, but were simply revived and returned to use as daily equipment. However, they are the very roots of kintsugi.

In the past (in an era without mass production and mass consumption), there were only a few bowls and teacups in the home, so craftsmen went around to each household to repair them. I often repair tea bowls and teacups using kasugai techniques (repair that connects vessels with something like a staple made of bamboo or metal). Many people come to my studio in Kyoto and say, "In the old days, there were many tea bowls and teacups like this," and return home with feelings of nostalgia after seeing the kasugai. The unpretentious handmade repairs make people feel relaxed. It is often said that a child is a blessing in disguise, and the analogy of a child strengthening the bond between a husband and wife may have been born from family conversations over meals with such repaired bowls.

職人の世界
漆文化のはじまり、大陸文化との出会い

　第1章で、漆による修復や装飾が縄文時代から行われてきたことを述べました。時が過ぎて、平安時代の末頃に編まれた、日本で最初の国語辞典『色葉字類抄』では、漆と人間の出会いについて、日本武尊が大和国宇陀（奈良県宇陀郡）の阿賀山中に狩猟に出かけた際、偶然漆を発見し、後に漆を司る政庁を置いたというエピソードが残されています。

　飛鳥から奈良時代にかけて、日本は隋や唐といった超大国の影響下にありました。漆芸の分野もその例外ではなく、6世紀の後半、大陸の新しい技術が朝鮮半島を経由して入ってきます。現在、奈良・東大寺の正倉院に保管されている、螺鈿や金銀絵などの様々な技法で飾られた漆芸品は、1200年もの遥か昔につくられたことが信じられないほど良好な状態を保っており、そこに施された高度な技術、洗練された表現を目の当たりにした時、現代の私たちも感動を覚えずにはいられません。

　様々な大陸文化に触れた当時の日本人も、最初はあまりの迫力に圧倒される思いだったでしょう。しかし職人は、直ちに大陸の技法を学んで自分たちのものとし、さらに「蒔絵」という優れた装飾技術を生み出すに至ったのです。

　そこに行きつくには、多くの職人たちの血のにじむような努力、試行錯誤が積み重ねられたに違いありません。ただ、短期間に日本の漆芸が飛躍的な発展を遂げた背景には、漆が日本で永く愛用されてきた素材であるということ、そして漆器が人々の心に響く存在であったことを忘れてはならないと思います。

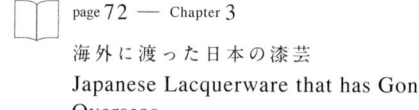

page 72 ― Chapter 3
海外に渡った日本の漆芸
Japanese Lacquerware that has Gone Overseas

The Craftsman's World

The Beginning of Urushi Culture, Encounters with Continental Culture

In the section on the history of lacquer in Chapter 1, I mentioned that urushi-based restoration and decoration has been practiced in Japan since the Jomon period. The first Japanese language dictionary, *Irohaji-ruisho*, compiled around the end of the Heian period (794–1185), mentions the first encounter between urushi and mankind as follows: "Yamato Takeru no Mikoto, on a hunting trip to the Aga Mountains in Uda, Yamato Province (Uda-gun, Nara Prefecture), happened to discover urushi."

From the Asuka to Nara periods, Japan was under the influence of the superpowers of the Sui and Tang dynasties. In the latter half of the 6th century, new techniques from the continent were introduced via the Korean Peninsula. The lacquerware decorated with such techniques such as mother-of-pearl inlays, gold and silver painting, etc., currently stored in the Shosoin Repository are in such good condition that it is hard to believe that they were made 1,200 years ago.

The Japanese people of that time, who were exposed to various continental cultures, must have been overwhelmed by the sheer power of those cultures at first. However, the craftmen of that time soon learned the techniques of the continent, made them their own, and created an excellent original decorative technique called "maki-e."

It must have taken a lot of hard work, trial and error by many craftsmen, to achieve that. However, we should not forget that the lacquer art of Japan was able to develop so amazingly within a short period of time because urushi was a material long used in Japan, and lacquerware was something that resonated with people's hearts.

職人の世界
徒弟制度と御礼奉公

　私が修業した時、まず2年以上は師匠の身辺の世話だけをさせられました。家の掃除から、自転車のスポークまで毎日磨いていたのです。漆の作業部屋への入室を許されたのは、なんと4年目のことでした。作業部屋に上げてもらう前、師匠に呼ばれ、めずらしくお茶を振る舞ってもらいました。飲み終わった後、「明日から1週間休んでいいぞ」と言われ、「やった。1週間休めるのか」と思ったら翌日からかぶれと発熱が続きました。実は湯呑みには、漆が塗ってあったのです。漆のかぶれが引くのがちょうど1週間くらいです。師匠の仕業は、漆と一生向き合う覚悟を持っているのかという、いわば弟子に対する意思確認でした。師匠は私が1週間後に自分の元に現れるかどうかで、弟子になれる見込みを判断したのでした。

　現在、徒弟制度はほとんどなく、例えば漆芸であれば、大学の漆芸科、美術科で勉強された方が、長い修業経験を持たずに職に就く時代です。もちろん、それは悪いことではありませんが、振り返ってみると、漆に人生を懸ける気概があるかを判断するためには、あの苦しい1週間は私には必要だったのかもしれません。

　修業中に手取り足取り教えられると、それ以上のことを想像できなくなります。教えられるのではなく見て覚えることで、私だったらああするのに、という創造力が養われます。若い頃は、師匠に対していつも腹が立っていましたが、考えてみるに師匠の本意は「自分を超えてくれ」というものだったのでしょう。

　また、御礼奉公という文化もありました。御礼奉公とは、これまでの恩返しとして、師匠の仕事を安価で手伝うことです。いつでも相談できるようにパイプを繋いでおく、という師匠の計らいが御礼奉公でした。当時はいつまで奉公させられるのかと思いましたが、実は師匠の気遣いだったのです。同時に御礼奉公は、今はなくなりつつある、日本の技術承継の方法のひとつでもありました。

The Craftsman's World

The Apprentice System and Service Work

When I started my apprenticeship, I was required to take care of my master's personal needs for at least two years. I had to clean his house and even polish the spokes of his bicycle every day. It wasn't until my fourth year that I was allowed to enter the urushi workroom. Before I was allowed to enter the room, my master called me over and served me a cup of tea, which was a very rare occurrence. Actually, the bottom of my teacup had been freshly lacquered. After I finished drinking the tea, I was told that I could take a week off from the next day, which I thought was great, but the next day I came down with a fever and broke out in a rash. It took exactly one week for the urushi rash to go away. My master's actions were to confirm whether I was ready to face urushi for the rest of my life, so to speak. He judged my chances of becoming an apprentice based on whether or not I would show up at his place after that rather unpleasant week.

Today, there is almost no apprentice system, and in the case of lacquerware, for example, people who have studied lacquerware or fine arts at university can get a job without a long period of training. Of course, there is nothing wrong with that, but in retrospect, I think I needed that painful week to determine whether I had the determination to devote my life to urushi.

Once you are instructed by the master with great attention to detail during your training, it is hard to create anything original. But by learning from observation instead of being taught, we can develop our creativity. We grow to think of what we would do if we were the master. When I was young, I used to get angry at my teachers, but I guess their intention was to make me surpass them.

There was also the culture of orei-boko "gratitude service". The term "orei-boko" means to work for a master at a low wage as a way of repaying him for what he has done for you up to now. Orei-boko also was a way for the master to connect with the work interns so that they could consult with him at any time. At the time, I wondered how long I would be forced to do this service work for my master, but it was all actually his expression of concern for me. Orei-boko certainly worked as a way of passing on Japanese craftman skills, and the transmission of those skills is in many cases now disappearing.

Photo | page 36-37

師匠から譲り受けた道具類
Tools passed down to me from my master

職人の世界
職人文化の衰退への危機感

　日本文化は先人たちの独特の感性によって育(はぐく)まれ、すばらしい「ものづくり」を追求してきました。そしてそれだけではなく、先人の職人たちは、ものづくりを通して培(つちか)った技法を、後世に伝えることを忘れませんでした。しかし、近年の大量生産・大量消費の動きは、人々のものへの想いを大きく変えてしまいました。職人が江戸時代から続く技術を持っていても、それで稼げる機会が少なくなり、将来の展望が見えなくなると、彼らの後継者育成も難しくなってきました。

　私が行う漆芸修復の仕事を例にとると、漆芸は、漆の木を育てる職人、漆掻きをする職人、漆を精製する職人、そして彼らが使用する多様な道具をつくる職人たちがいて初めて成立するものです。どの職人が欠けても私の仕事は成立しないのです。

The Craftsman's World

A Sense of Crisis Over the Decline of Craftsman Culture

Japanese culture has been nurtured by the unique sensibility of our ancestors, who pursued the art of creating wonderful objects. Not only that, but the craftsmen of the past never forgot to pass on to future generations the techniques they cultivated in that pursuit of theirs. However, in recent years, mass production and mass consumption have greatly changed the way people think about things. Even if craftsmen have skills that have lasted since the Edo period, the opportunities to earn money from them have diminished, and it has become difficult to find successors for them as their future prospects become uncertain.

Taking my work in urushi lacquer restoration as an example, my restoration is only possible because of specialists who grow urushi trees, those who collect the sap from the trees, and those who refine the urushi. If any one of these specialists were missing, my restoration would not be possible. By the way, I have always believed that a good craftsman lets his tools do the work. In the past, in order to make good tools, the lacquer art crafting process was divided among different

また、私は「優れた職人は道具に仕事をさせる」と常々思っています。昔は、良い道具づくりのために、筆をつくる人、筆を洗う人、色を塗る人、線を描く人など、工程は各職人に分業され、それぞれが切磋琢磨していました。つまり、各作業にスペシャリストがいた時代で、皆、人より腕を磨いて、より良いポジションを摑もうと虎視眈々としていました。現在、このような職人の分業制は少なくなりつつあります。

　私が使う筆は、京都の大原にある創業300年の京都を代表する筆工房に依頼しています。この筆工房の面相筆は、毛先に天然イタチの毛を用い、軸は大原の竹で設えた手づくりの一本です。この筆は漆に実によくなじみ、繊細で細い線を描くことができます。工房は責任者である筆職人が奥様と一緒に営んでおられ、現在職人は70歳を超えていますが、後継者がいないのです。もし彼が引退したら、彼と同じレベルの筆をつくる職人は日本に一人も存在しません。なぜ後継者がいないのかというと、手づくりの和筆の需要が激減して、商売にならないからです。私の仕事の背景には、使う道具や漆をつくる多くの職人が存在しています。彼らが仕事を縮小している現在、私は日本の伝統工芸の衰退に大きな危機感を抱いています。海外で高い評価を得ている日本の伝統工芸が、実は人知れず消えていこうとしているのが現状です。

　実は私自身も弟子を取っていないため、私が45年間積み上げた技術の正統な後継者がいるのかと問われると、後継者はいないのです。ただ、私は自分が教える金継ぎ教室の生徒や工房で働いてくれるスタッフに、知り得る技術をできる限り教授しています。彼らの中から、より深く勉強したい人たちが現れたり、私の元で学んでくれた人が地元で教室を開いてくれたりすることが、伝統技法の承継において最も大事だと思っています。私が主な仕事を文化財修復から金継ぎ修復に移行しているのは、金継ぎ修復が生活から生まれた伝統文化であり、人々が取り組みやすい技法であるからです。私は伝統技法への理解とその承継を、これからも金継ぎ修復を通じて広く行っていきたいと思っています。

specialists: those who made the brushes, those who washed the brushes, those who painted the colors, and those who drew the lines. It was a time when there was a specialist for each task, and everyone watched vigilantly to improve their skills and get a better position. Today, this division of labor is disappearing.

The brushes I use are made by a brush studio in Ohara, Kyoto, that has been in business for 300 years. The brushes are handmade using natural weasel hair for the tips and bamboo from Ohara for the shaft. This brush blends really well with lacquer and allows me to draw delicate lines. The brush craftsman who is responsible for the workshop runs it with his wife. He is now over 70 years old and has no successor. Once he retires, there will not be a single craftsman in Japan who can produce brushes of the same level of quality as he does. The reason why there are no successors is because the demand for handmade Japanese brushes has plummeted, making it impossible to do business. The background of my work requires many specialists who make the tools and lacquer I use. Now that they are folding up their businesses, I have a great sense of crisis about the decline of traditional Japanese crafts. These traditions, which are highly regarded overseas, are actually threatened at their core.

As a matter of fact, I myself have not taken any apprentices, so if you ask whether a legitimate successor to the skills and knowledge I have accumulated over the past 45 years is in place, I answer that no such person is in place. I have no successor. However, I try to teach as much as I can about the techniques I know to the students in my kintsugi classes and the staff who work in my studio. I believe that the most important thing for the effective succession of traditional techniques is for people who have learned from me to want to study more deeply. I also hope that among those who have learned from me some would open their own studios locally. I have shifted my main work from the restoration of cultural properties to the restoration of kintsugi, because kintsugi restoration is a traditional culture born from daily life, and it is a technique that people can easily work with, even today. For this reason I would like to continue to promote the understanding of traditional techniques and their succession through kintsugi restoration.

職人の世界 | The Craftsman's World

修復職人としての心構え
A Restorer's Attitude

　仏像や陶磁器などの古いものを修復する際、私はそれがどのような時代にどのような素材でつくられたのかを見極めて、可能な限り当時の技法と材料で仕上げます。

　私はよく江戸時代につくられたそば猪口(ちょく)を修復する機会を持ちます。あるそば猪口は二つに割れ、すでに接着剤で修復されていましたが、持ち主の方が制作当時の方法で修復し直したいとの要望でした。そこでまず、そば猪口を水から沸騰(ふっとう)させ、沸騰直前に取り出して接着部分を外し、次に「のり漆」で接着して「錆漆(さびうるし)」を盛り、割れた部分を覆(おお)いました。この後、「錆漆」の上に黒漆で中塗り、上塗りのコーティングを行い防水効果を持たせてから、弁柄(べんがら)漆(うるし)を塗って金を蒔(ま)きました。

　このそば猪口は、「割れ」から新しい景色を得て蘇(よみがえ)りました。この修復にかかっ

When restoring an old object, I try to determine the procedure by which it was made, and then to use the techniques and materials original to it as much as possible.

I often have the opportunity to restore Edo-period soba-choku (cups used for eating buckwheat noodles). One such cup was broken in two and had already been repaired with glue. The owner wanted me to repair it using the traditional method. First, I put the cup in water which I then brought to near boiling point, and removed the glued part. After that, we glued it with nori-urushi and covered the cracks with sabi-urushi. After this process, I coated it with black lacquer and gold lacquer.

This soba-choku was reborn with a new look and feel achieved by the "break." The restoration work took about three months. Whenever I am asked to restore an old piece like this, I think how luxurious it is to be able to restore a piece of pottery that is over 100 years old. I feel as if I am having a dialogue with the craftsman who created the piece back

打宅公軌像修復のようす（妙光寺蔵）
Restoration of the Uda Kimnori Statue (Myokoji Temple)

た期間はおよそ3か月。私はこのような古い作品の修復を頼まれる度、100年以上前の器を修復させていただくのは、なんと贅沢(ぜいたく)なひと時だろうと思います。時を超えて、まるで当時作品をつくった職人と対話をしているような感覚になるのです。そしてただ修復するのではなく、その技法を後世に繋げていくことを心がけています。

then. In addition, I do not just restore the pieces, but try to pass on the techniques to future generations.

In general, technology gets more advanced as time moves forward. However, I have been doing this work for 45 years, and I feel that I cannot compete with the high level of skill of the craftsmen of the Edo period. The power of their work is different. For me, the craftsmen of the Edo period are my rivals. I would like

一般的に、未来の方が技術は発展しているものです。しかし、45年この仕事を続けていても、江戸時代の職人の技術の高さには敵（かな）わないと感じます。仕事の「迫力」が違うのです。私にとっては江戸時代の職人こそがライバルです。だからせめて、お預かりしたものから先人の技や心を学び、自分が修復することでそれらを後世に伝えていきたいと思っています。

　修復では、少しでも手を抜いてしまうと、その修復がそのまま後世に残ることになり、やがて「常識」になってしまう可能性があります。また、現代人の解釈を主体にして修復を行うと、昔の職人の技術や感性が正しく理解されず、国を代表する文化遺産でさえ、違う様相になってしまいます。昨今、世界中で修復前と修復後があまりに異なるケースがあり、批判の声が上がっています。

　先人の創作を正しく後世に伝えるためには、熟練の職人が多くいて、さらに彼らの切磋琢磨が必要です。また、修復の際には当時の風合いを残すことも大切です。なぜなら、すべてをきれいに直すとそれは「今」の作品になってしまうからです。「職人が古来伝わる技法で修復を行い、可能な限り元の姿に復元して、同時にその時代の職人の感性をも未来に承継すること」が、修復師の心構えであると私は思っています。

to at least learn the skills, and perhaps also acquaint myself with the mindsets, of my predecessors from the objects placed in my care. By my restoring them, I can pass this knowledge on to future generations.

In the process of passing on techniques through restoration, if we cut corners even a little in the restoration process, that work will remain for future generations and may unfortunately become a common model. In addition, if restoration is done mainly based on the interpretation of modern people, the techniques and sensibilities of the craftsmen of the past will not be properly understood. In this way, even the cultural heritage that represents the country can be lost or obscured. In recent years, criticism has arisen because of the cases around the world where in restored works have been much too different from the original.

In order to faithfully pass works produced by our predecessors on to future generations, many skilled craftspeople need to work hard. It is important to preserve the original texture when restoring. It is also important to preserve the original look and feel of the piece. If everything is repaired too cleanly, too efficiently, it becomes merely a work of the present. I believe that the motivation of the restorer should be to return a piece to its original state as much as possible, by using techniques that have been handed down from generation to generation. At the same time, the restorer should try to pass on the sensitivity of the craftsmen of that era to the future.

職人の世界
千年の釘にいどむ

　1981年の奈良・薬師寺西塔再建にまつわる「千年の釘にいどむ」という話があります。薬師寺西塔は今から1000年以上前の奈良時代に建てられたものです。西塔再建には、宮大工・西岡常一氏を棟梁に、日本全国から一流の職人が集められました。その中に、「和釘」の職人・白鷹幸伯氏がいました。

　白鷹氏は、再建後からの1000年に向けて寺を支え続ける釘は、現代の一般的な釘ではなく、古来の方法でつくられた釘を用いるべきだと考え、試行錯誤を重ねました。一般的な釘は、頭から下は同じ太さで、先端に向けて徐々に細くなっていきます。一方、古来使われていた釘は胴部分が太く、その上は細いつくりになっています。

　この釘を檜に打ち込むと、檜には胴と同じ大きさの穴が開き、釘の首の周りに隙間ができてしまいます。ところが、檜の繊維は元の形に戻る性質があるので、時間が経つと膨らんで、隙間を埋めてしまうのです。その結果、太い胴部分が締めつけられ、抜けなくなるのです。白鷹氏は、この先人の知恵を用いた釘を復元しようと、納得がいくまで実に2万4000本もの釘をつくりました。製鉄会社に頼み込んで、奈良時代と同じ純度の高い鉄をつくってもらい、釘の微妙なフォルムを追求し続けました。

　後に白鷹氏は次のように語ったそうです。「千年後の鍛冶職人に、千年前のやつは下手くそだと笑われるのは嫌だ。これは職人としての意地だ」。

　白鷹氏は1000年前に使われた釘を通して、1000年前の職人と対話し、自分の職人生命の全てをかけて釘をつくり、1000年後の鍛冶職人に結果を託しました。彼は1000年の時を駆けるタイムトラベラーであり、私もまた金継ぎをしながら、修復される器がたどってきた時の流れを感じています。私も白鷹氏のように、1000年後の誰かに誇れる仕事をする、その覚悟をもって修復を行う職人でありたいと思っています。

The Craftsman's World

Meeting the Challenge of a Thousand-year-old Nail

There is a story about the reconstruction of the West Pagoda at Yakushiji Temple in Nara Prefecture that took place in 1981, called "The Thousand-Year-Old Nail." Yakushiji Temple was built more than 1,000 years ago, in the Nara period (710–794). For the 1981 reconstruction of its West Pagoda, top-notch craftsmen from all over Japan were gathered under the supervision of Tsunekazu Nishioka, a shrine carpenter. One of them was Mr. Yukinori Shirataka, a specialist in the field of tradition-style Japanese nails.

Mr. Shirataka went through an intense trial and error process to reproduce nails of the same quality as those used in the original construction. He wanted to use nails made the ancient way, instead of modern common nails, to support the temple for another thousand years. Generally, modern nails are the same thickness from the head down, and gradually become thinner toward the tip. The nails used in ancient times, however, are thicker at the body and thinner at the top. When this nail is driven into the cypress, a hole the same size as the nail body is made in the cypress, and a gap is created around the neck. However, the cypress fibers have a tendency to return to their original shape, so over time they swell and tighten around the neck of the nail. As a result, the thick body of the nail becomes constricted and cannot be pulled out. Mr. Shirataka made 24,000 of these nails until he was satisfied that he could remake the nails using the wisdom and techniques of our ancestors. Continuing his pursuit of the ideal subtle form, he asked an iron manufacturing company to produce iron of the same high purity as in the Nara period, for exclusive use in producing the nails.

Mr. Shirataka later said, "I don't want to be laughed at by future blacksmiths a thousand years from now. I have principles as a craftsman."

Through the nails used 1,000 years ago, Mr. Shirataka was able to communicate with the blacksmith of 1,000 years ago. As a dedicated craftsman, he put his whole into making the nails, and entrusted the results to the blacksmiths of 1,000 years from now. He is a time traveler sprinting across a millennia. I am also moving through time as I restore things by kintsugi. Like Mr. Shirataka, I would like to be a craftsman with the determination to restore artwork that someone else can be proud of a thousand years from now.

職人の世界
金箔を貼る

　私は30代半ばから40代にかけて、寺院本堂内内陣の正面長押に金箔を貼る修復に携わっていました。長押は、外陣と内陣の結界の役目を果たしています。結界とは、神社仏閣における聖なる場所（内陣）と俗なる場所（外陣）とを分ける境目のことで、仏教では寺院の境内の奥に「聖域」として内陣がつくられます。内陣とはいわゆる極楽浄土であり、外陣は現世（俗世）と考えられています。

　正面長押の金箔貼りは、どんな職人にもできるものではありません。私は幸運にも30代に寺院の修復で最も大事な金箔貼りを請け負い、高僧でも年に数回しか入ることのできない内陣に長期間入れていただくことができました。

　長押修復は、まず傷んだ金箔と上漆、その下にある麻布と錆漆を剝がす作業から始まります。200年以上経った漆を剝がし、下地を落として、長押を丸裸の材木にします。この工程を「掻き落とし」といいます。その後、丸裸の長押を再び麻布で包み、上に錆漆を均等に塗りつけます。麻で包む理由は、麻布の伸縮性が上に乗せる錆漆のひび割れを防ぐためです。麻布の上で錆漆が硬化したら表面を研いで滑らかにし、そこに数回に分けて下地漆塗りを行い、最後に膠と漆でつくった箔漆を塗って、それが乾ききる前に金箔を貼ります。

　さて、本堂内の内陣の、最も大事な正面長押を飾る金箔を貼る作業についてです。長押は極楽浄土と現世を分ける結界であるため、魔よけの意味もある「金箔」は、鮮やかな輝きがむらなく連続するように、かつ長押の端から端まで1ミリの隙間を空けることなく、貼りつけなければなりません。箔が途中で曲がったり、しわになったり、破れたり、隣同士がずれたりしてはいけないのです。

　また、金箔の厚みは、1万分の2ミリしかありません。金箔は、人の呼吸や咳払いでも破れて飛んで行ってしまうほど繊細な

The Craftsman's World
Gold Leafing

From my mid-thirties to my forties, I was involved in the restoration of gold leaf on the nageshi transoms at the front of the inner sanctuary of the main hall of a temple. The nageshi transoms serve as a boundary between the outer and inner sanctuaries. In Buddhism, the inner sanctuary is built deep within the temple grounds as a sacred space. The inner sanctuary is the so-called Pure Land, while the outer sanctuary represents the worldly realm.

The gilding of the front nageshi is not something that any craftsman can do. I was fortunate enough in my thirties to be entrusted with this most important part of temple restoration, the gilding, and was able to spend a long time in the inner sanctuary, which even high priests are only allowed to enter a few times a year.

The first step in restoring a nageshi is to remove the urushi and base coat. The urushi, which is more than 200 years old, is stripped away and the base is removed, leaving the nageshi as a bare piece of wood. This process is called kakiotoshi, "scratching off." The wood is then wrapped in hemp cloth and coated evenly with sabi-urushi lacquer. The reason for wrapping the wood in hemp cloth is that its elasticity the prevents the sabi-urushi on top from cracking. After the sabi-urushi has hardened on the hemp, the surface is polished to make it smooth, and then the base lacquer is applied several times.

Next I will describe the process of applying the all-important gold leaf which decorates the nageshi of the inner sanctuary of the temple's main hall. As I mentioned earlier, the nageshi is the boundary between the Pure Land and this world, so the gold leaf, which is also meant to ward off evil, must be applied evenly and continuously, without leaving a gap of even a millimeter from one end of the nageshi to the other. The foil must not be bent, wrinkled, torn, or misaligned.

Moreover, the thickness of gold leaf is only two thousandths of a millimeter. Gold leaf is such a delicate material that even a person's breath or a cough can rend it to pieces and send it flying. The thinner the gold leaf, the easier it is for the gold particles to penetrate into the lacquer particles, thus the ultra-thin preparation. The foil lacquer dries within 30 minutes to an hour, depending on the size of the nageshi. Therefore, once the foil lacquer is applied to the

素材です。

　金箔が極めて薄い理由は、薄ければ薄いほど金の粒子が漆の粒子に入り込みやすいからです。金箔貼りの前に膠が混入された箔漆を塗るのは、箔漆が金箔の吸着に最適なのです。箔漆が乾くスピードは、長押の大きさにもよりますが、30分から1時間ほどです。ですから、一旦箔漆を長押に塗ったら、もう作業を引き返すことはできません。私は極限まで集中力を高めて、特別な竹のピンセットで金箔をつまんで、箔漆の上に載せていきます。

　漆が最良の状態で乾くには、適切な温度と湿度が必要です。私は日々の温度・湿度をノートにつけて大気の傾向を読み、朝起きた時の空気の流れを肌に感じて、金箔を貼る日を決めます。当日、湿度が足りないと思ったら、本堂の天井から濡れた布巾をいくつも吊るして湿度を上げていきます。本堂そのものを、漆の室にしてしまうのです。

　足場を組み、適量の箔漆を用意し、作業板に乗せる金箔の枚数を揃えます。温度、湿度が良い状態になったと感じたら、いよいよ作業開始です。

　作業中は空気中に浮遊する塵や服についている糸くずなどの埃には格別の注意を払わなければなりません。寺の住職の方々が見学に来られますが、私は皆さんに「見学してもよいですが、絶対にしゃべらず、また動かないでください」とお願いします。

　薄い金箔を竹のピンセットでそっとつまんで目線まで持ち上げ、空気の流れに乗せると、私の手に運ばれた金箔は黄金の蝶のように目の前を横切って、箔漆が塗られた長押に張りつきます。

　修復中の私は空気の流れを「見る」ことができました。空中に漂う塵をよけ、気の流れに金箔を乗せながら、それを目的の場所にふわっと置いてあげます。それは蝶が羽を広げて花の上にふわっと止まる感じです。

　私は何も考えず、心を空っぽにして作業を続けます。隙間が空かないように隣の金箔に2ミリほど重ねるようにして貼り、金箔が上がったり下がったりしないように、己の水平感覚を信じて貼り続けます。

　全てが終了した時は、大きな疲労を感じますが、次の200年に繋げる修復に立ち向かった職人としての充実感も覚えます。そして、今日の自分の仕事が、200年前の職人と未来の職人に誇れるものであるかを自問自答しています。

nageshi, there is no turning back. With extreme concentration, I pick up the gold leaf with special bamboo tweezers and place it on the foil lacquer. (The reason for using bamboo tweezers is to prevent static electricity.)

In order for the lacquer to dry in the best condition, it needs the right humidity and temperature. In addition, we need to pay special attention to dust floating in the air and lint on our clothes. I keep a notebook of the daily temperature and humidity, read the atmospheric trends, feel the air flow when I wake up in the morning, and decide the day to apply the gold leaf. If I feel the air is not humid enough, I hang a number of wet clothes from the ceiling of the main hall to raise the humidity. The main hall itself is turned into a kind of muro (urushi drying chamber).

The scaffolding is erected, the right amount of foil lacquer prepared, and the necessary number of gold leaves, cut into 10 cm squares, has been assembled for setting on the work board. Once the temperature and humidity are confirmed as good, the work can begin.

While I am working, the priests of the temple come to observe, but I ask them not to talk or move, although they can watch quietly. The thin gold leaf, picked up with tweezers, crosses my line of sight and sticks to the lacquer.

During the restoration, I could see the flow of air. I could see the flow of air as I wafted the gold into place, dodging dust in the air and placing the gold leaf, fluffing it where I wanted it. The image is like a butterfly spreading its wings and perching on a flower.

I don't think about anything, I just empty my mind and keep working. I apply the gold leaf,

trusting my senses to make sure there are no gaps, and that the gold leaf does not rise or fall as I put it on.

When everything is finished, I am filled with great fatigue, but I also remember the sense of fulfillment as a craftsman who has finished a restoration that will last the next 200 years. I contemplate if my work today is something I can be proud of, considering the craftsmen of hundreds of years ago, and the craftsmen of the future.

高野教会のマリア像

　高野教会は京都市左京区にあるカトリック教会です。近くを高野川が流れ、少し足を延ばすと下鴨神社があります。2013年5月、私はこの教会の信者の方より、前庭に立っている聖母マリア像の修復を依頼されました。

　マリア像は、韓国で布教をされていたバーン神父が1940年に日本に着任するにあたり、韓国から運んできたもので、その時点ですでに30年ほど経過していました。像は石膏でつくられており、長年雨ざらしで置かれていたため、ひどく劣化していました。それまでは、教会の信者さんがペンキを塗ってしのいできましたが、近年は聖母マリアのお顔も胴体も傷みが激しく、思い切って撤去すべきという声もあったそうです。

　しかし、このマリア像は高野教会の信仰の証であり、バーン神父の布教の礎(いしずえ)であったことから、何とか保存したいということで、私に修復の相談が入りました。

　私は漆芸で神社仏閣にある仏像や調度品の修復はしたことがあっても、石膏像の修復は初めてです。それでも信者さんの想いに導かれるように教会に出向き、マリア像を見た時、私は修復を決意しました。

The Statue of Mary at Takano Church

Takano Church is a Catholic church located in Sakyo-ku, Kyoto. The Takano River flows nearby, and Shimogamo Shrine is a few steps away.

In May 2013, I was asked by a member of this church to repair the statue of the Virgin Mary standing in the front yard. The statue of Mary had been brought from Korea by Father Barnes, a missionary there, when he arrived in Japan in 1940. The statue was made of plaster and had been left in the rain for many years, so it had deteriorated badly. The church members had painted the statue from time to time, but in recent years both the face and body of the statue had become so seriously damaged, some people thought the statue should be removed. However, since this statue of Mary was a testimony of the faith of Takano Church and the foundation of Father Burns' missionary work, church members wanted to preserve it somehow, and asked me for advice on its restoration.

My field is urushi lacquerware, and I have restored Buddhist statues and furnishings in shrines and temples, but this would be my first time restoring a plaster statue. Nevertheless, as if guided by the thoughts of believers, I went to the church, and when I saw the statue of Mary, I decided to restore it. In addition to the gentle face of Mary, which was tattered from the rain and wind, I noticed her feet peeking out from the hem. In spite of her gentle face, her legs were as big and strong as a man's. She seemed to be watching over the church as if she were a mother figure with her roots planted in the earth.

I was moved by the image of Mary standing like a guardian deity.

The methods of lacquer restoration I knew so well could be used for the restoration of the statue, although the materials would be different. I would begin by peeling off all the layers of paint that had been applied to the statue over the years.

　雨風に耐えてぼろぼろになっていた聖母マリアの顔が優しかったことに加え、裾（すそ）から覗（のぞ）いている聖母マリアの足に目が行きました。優しい顔なのに、足は男性のように大きくて逞（たくま）しく、母なる存在として大地に根を張って教会を見守っているかのようでした。

　私は、守護神のごとく佇（たたず）む聖母マリアの姿に心を動かされたのです。

　像の修復は、材料は異なるものの、これまでに習得した漆芸修復と同じ工法で行いました。まず、歴年の間にマリア像に上塗りされたペンキを剥がすことから始めました。

　私は、次の100年にマリア像を託（たく）すのは自分たち大人ではなく子供たちだと考え、日曜学校に通う子供たちに手伝いを頼むことにしました。ペンキを剥がした思い出を持ってもらうことで、将来、子供たちが教会運営の中心となった時、マリア像を大事にしてほしいと思ったのです。

　ペンキを剥がし終えたマリア像を寒冷紗（かんれいしゃ）という布で覆（おお）い、その上に石膏を重ね塗りして土台を作った後、顔と衣服の再生に取りかかりました。寒冷紗は、粗く平織に織り込んだ布で、織り糸には麻や綿が使われます。伸縮性があり、下地に使うことで温度・湿度による石膏の表層のひび割れを抑える効果があります。

　さて、衣服は順調に修復できましたが、私が悩んだのは聖母マリアの顔でした。

　次の100年、聖母マリアは京都の信者さんをどのような表情で見守るのか、考え抜いた末、私はアルカイク・スマイルを湛（たた）えたマリア様をつくりたいと思いました。アルカイク・スマイルは古代ギリシャのアルカイク美術の彫像に見られる表情で、紀元前6世紀後半の作に例が多いものです。顔の感情表現を極力抑えながら、口元だけは微笑む形を伴（とも）っているのが特徴で、生命感と幸福感を顕（あらわ）す表情といわれています。日本語では「古拙の微笑（こせつのほほえみ）」の意味で、「古拙」は素朴で古風な味わいといったところです。日本では飛鳥時代につくられた仏像がアルカイク・スマイルの特徴をとらえています。京都・広隆寺（こうりゅうじ）の木造弥勒菩薩半跏（もくぞうみろくぼさつはんか）思惟像（しゆい）（宝冠弥勒（ほうかんみろく））や奈良・中宮寺（ちゅうぐうじ）の菩薩半跏像（ぼさつはんかぞう）（弥勒菩薩）などが有名です。

　頭の中には聖母マリアの顔のイメージがしっかりできているのですが、それを実際につくり上げるのは至難（しなん）の業（わざ）でした。5月に修復依頼を受け、6月から8月の真夏に行った作業は大変でしたが、制作している間、

I thought to make a project of it, and asked the Sunday school students to help me. I reasoned that it would be the children of the present congregation, not the adults, who would care for the statue for the next 100 years. I hoped that the memory of carefully removing the paint from the damaged Mary would inspire the children to take good care of the statue in the future, when they become the core of the church management.

We covered the painted statue with cheesecloth, and after building a base by applying layers of plaster, we began to recreate the face and clothing. Cheesecloth is a cloth woven into a rough plain weave. Hemp or cotton is used for the weaving thread. The cloth has elasticity, and when used as a base, is effective in preventing surface plaster from cracking due to temperature and humidity.

Although I was able to restore Mary's garment, her face still troubled me.

After much deliberation, I decided that I wanted to create a Mary with an Archaic smile. The Archaic smile is an expression found on statues of Archaic art in ancient Greece, with many examples in the late 6th century BC. It is characterized by the fact that only the mouth expresses the shape of a smile, while the expression of emotion on the face is kept to a minimum. The smile manifests a sense of fullness of life and well-being. In Japanese, the term for this would be "kosetsu no hohoemi" (calm old smile), the word "kosetsu" suggesting something simple, timeless. In Japan, Buddhist statues made in the Asuka period have the characteristics of an archaic smile. The most famous examples are the Maitreya Bodhisattva (Maitreya with a Crowned Head) at Koryuji Temple, and the Maitreya Bodhisattva at Chuguji Temple, both in Nara Prefecture.

I had a clear image of the face in my mind, but it was extremely difficult to actually create it. I was asked to restore the statue in May and the work was done in the middle of summer, from June to August. It was a lot of work. When I had completed my third retrial of the face, I noticed that the churchgoers would join their hands when seeing the statue. After they placed their hands on the statue, they bowed deeply to me as I was restoring it. Seeing the devotees, I felt that I had created what I thought was an Archaic smile, so I stopped my work. I decorated the edge of the veil that Mary wears with gold, as a charm to ward off evil, and called it done.

There is a later story about the restoration of the statue of Mary. The daughter of one of the churchgoers had been ill for a long time, and passed away just as the restoration of the statue was completed. After seeing to her daughter's final affairs, her mother came to me and said, "Mary's face looks so much like my daughter's face. It was as if she had come to see us from heaven, to watch over us." Her words were a kind of revelation and strengthened my resolve as a long-time restoration craftsman.

All restorations must be done in a way that responds to the wishes of those who are left behind and will inherit the work and care for it, and I must accept those wishes and move my hands. The restoration of the statue of Mary was an unforgettable experience for me.

　私はマリア像100年目にして初めての修復を手がけられた職人としての喜びをかみしめていました。
　つくってはやり直して、3回目の顔が完成した時、私は教会を訪れる幾人かの信者さんがマリア像に手を合わせてくれることに気づきました。信者さんはマリア像に手を合わせた後、修復している私にも深く礼をしてくださいました。
　私は信者さんたちの姿を見て、私の思うアルカイク・スマイルができたことを感じて作業をやめ、最後に邪悪を退けるお守りの意味を込めて、聖母マリアが被るベールの縁を金で装飾しました。
　マリア像の修復には後日談があります。実は、ある信者さんのお嬢様が長く闘病を続けられた末、マリア像の修復が完成した頃に、天国に旅立たれました。お嬢様を見送られたお母様が私のところに来て、「マリア様のお顔が、娘の顔によく似ています。まるで亡くなった娘が私たちのことを見守るために、天国から会いにきてくれたように思いました」と話してくれたのです。修復を長年行ってきた私は、お母様の言葉を受けて、職人としての覚悟を決めました。
　全ての修復は、残された方や引き継いでいく方の思いに応えるように行わねばならず、その想いを受け止めて自分の手を動かすのだという覚悟と、運命が私に与えてくれたこの世での自分の役割についての覚悟です。
　マリア像の修復は、私のとって忘れられないものとなりました。

三章 ｜ Chapter 3

繕うこと、
その精神性と文化、
世界とのつながり

The World around
Kintsugi Restoration

繕うこと、その精神性と文化、世界とのつながり | The World around Kintsugi Restoration

私の考える茶道と繕い ── 利休と織部に思う
My Thoughts on Chado and Restoration: Rikyu and Oribe

　私はかねてから、戦国時代の茶人である千利休と古田織部に惹かれていました。千利休は、茶道の精神性を追求し、粗末でつつましい茶室の風情を好み、不必要な加飾は全て削ぎ落として「侘び」の世界をつくりました。

　利休は無駄に道具を持ちませんでした。それでも彼が愛用した「利休好み」と呼ばれる品々は、そのストイックさから多くの武将の人気を得ます。人為的につくられたものではなく、自然なものに価値を見出す利休の美意識が示したのは「新しい茶の湯」であり、身分や主従にとらわれず、ただ「生きていること」に感謝する心でした。その点で、権勢を示すために「黄金の茶室」をつくり、茶会を己の政治に利用した豊臣秀吉とは一線を画しています。

　私はまず、利休の道具を厳選する姿勢に惹かれました。「釜一つあれば茶の湯はなるものを　数の道具を持つは愚な」とは利休の言葉ですが、私も若い頃、師匠か

I have long been fascinated by Sen no Rikyu and Furuta Oribe, two tea masters from the Warring States period. Sen no Rikyu pursued the spirituality of chado (the "way of tea") and preferred the simple and unadorned atmosphere of a tea room. He created the world of wabi by first eliminating all unnecessary ornamentation. In addition, Rikyu did not possess any unnecessary tea implements.

Even so, his most beloved items, called "Rikyu's favorites," were admired by many warlords as well, because of the stoic aesthetic quality that the items possessed. Rikyu's aesthetic sense found beauty and value in natural things rather than artificially created things, and paved the way for a "new" kind of tea ceremony, one that was not bound by status or master/subordinate relationships, but which rather emphasized expression of a simple gratefulness to be alive. In this respect, Rikyu was a world apart from Toyotomi Hideyoshi, who built a gold tea house to display his power and used tea functions for political purposes.

The first thing that attracted me to Rikyu was his careful selection of tea implements. Once he said "A single kettle is all that is needed for the tea ceremony." Likewise, when I was young,

ら「道具は選んで持て。作業場を散らかしてはいけない」とさんざん言われました。後に私は、自分が選び抜いた道具に仕事をしてもらう、言い換えると、道具に仕事をさせることが大事であることを経験から学びました。

　また、利休は「割れた茶碗も風情です」と言っています。普段私たちは茶碗が欠けたら使わずに捨てますが、この言葉は、割れたものや不完全なものにこそ美があるという「侘び茶」の考えからきています。すすんで茶碗の割れ欠けをつくるということではなく、そのまま自然であることが良いという考えです。壊れることを自然なこととして受け入れ、それを隠さないという考えは、まさに金継ぎ修復と一緒です。

　もう1つ、あまりにも有名な利休の教えに「一期一会」があります。1回1回の茶席はたとえ同じ顔触れで席が催されたとしても、その全ての瞬間は一生に一度のことであり、もてなす方も招かれた方も誠心誠意で臨みなさい、という教えです。

　金継ぎ修復もまた一期一会の連続です。器の割れ欠けは毎回同じではなく、修復の仕方も異なります。器の持ち主とは、器を見舞ったアクシデントを通じて偶然的に出会いますが、私はいつも何らかのご縁を感じています。利休の「一期一会」は、1回1回の修復に真剣に向き合う姿勢がいかに大切であるかを、私に教えてくれました。

　古田織部は利休から「人と違うことをせよ」と教えを受け、利休亡き後、その茶道を継承しつつも、独力で織部流を確立します。彼は自然の美を求める一方で、自ら美を創り上げ、茶道具、建築、作庭などに執念を燃やし、「利休好み」に続いて「織部好み」と呼ばれる流れを創出しました。「織部好み」は慶長年間（1596～1615）に爆発的な流行となり、それは織部の亡後、約30年間も続きます。織部が用いた茶碗は、「へうげもの（ひょうきんなもの）」と言われ、激動の桃山時代後期に新しい文化を創出しました。

　私が最初に織部に興味を持ったのは、若い頃に彼の逸話つきの大井戸茶碗「須弥」（31頁）を見た時です。織部は茶碗が大き過ぎるのが気に入らず、十文字（四つ）に割り、削って継ぎ、小さくしたそうです。完成した茶碗をわざと壊して継ぎ合わせることで美しさを創造する「破調の美」に初めて触れ、自分の金継ぎ修復に「新たな1ページ」が加わりました。故意にものの「かたち」を捻じ曲げて生まれる偶然の美を楽しむ心、不調和の中に生まれる自然な落ち着き、即興的で抽象的な模様が描かれた茶碗から現れる前衛的感性、私は織部の「遊び」と「余裕」に羨望と尊敬の念を抱いたのです。金継ぎとは、単に器の割れ欠けを継ぐのではない、割れ欠けを「新しい景色」として解釈し、器の個性と向き合い、それを尊重しながらデザインして修復することなのだ、と思いを新たにしま

I was told by my urushi master, "Choose your tools carefully and don't make a mess in your workshop." Later, I learned from experience that it is important to let the tools you have selected do the work. In other words, it is important to make the tools do the work.

Rikyu also said, "A broken tea bowl is also tasteful." Normally, when a teacup is chipped, we stop using it and throw it away. However, this phrase comes from the notion of "wabicha," that there is beauty in broken and imperfect things. The idea is not to create cracks and chips in tea bowls by artifice, but simply to accept what has naturally happened. The idea of accepting breakage as a natural thing and not hiding it is exactly the same as the idea behind kintsugi restoration.

Another of Rikyu's most famous teachings is "Ichigo Ichie." These words mean that every encounter is precious and unique. Even if the same group of people attend a regularly occurring tea function, every time is a once-in-a-lifetime event, and both the host and the guest should be sincere, and should acknowledge the profundity of the encounter.

Kintsugi restoration is also a series of once-in-a-lifetime encounters. The cracks and chips in a vessel are not the same every time, and the method of restoration is appropriately different. Although I meet the owner of a vessel by chance through an accident, I always feel some kind of connection with him or her. Rikyu's "once-in-a-lifetime encounter" has taught me how important it is to take each restoration seriously.

Furuta Oribe was instructed by Rikyu to "do something different" in the tea world, and after Rikyu's death, Oribe established his own unique style while continuing to practice chado. Rather than seeking the beauty of nature, he created his own beauty and became obsessed with tea implements, architecture, and gardens. The "Oribe preference" became an explosive trend during the Keicho period (1596–1615), and continued for about 30 years after Oribe's death. The tea bowls used by Oribe were called hyoge-mono, "funny things," and created a new culture in the turbulent late Momoyama period.

I first became interested in Oribe when I was young and I saw his anecdotal large Ido tea bowl "Shumi (see page 31)." Oribe did not like that the tea bowl was too big, so he split it into four pieces, trimmed the pieces down, and joined them together again to make the bowl smaller. It was the first time that I came in contact with "the beauty of broken style" that creates aesthetic effect by intentionally breaking a tea bowl and joining the pieces together again, and a new page was added to my kintsugi restoration. I respected and was even a little envious of Oribe's playfulness. His generosity of spirit allowed him to enjoy the accidental beauty created by deliberately twisting the form of things, the natural calmness created in the incongrous, and the avant-garde sensibility that emerged from tea bowls with improvised and abstract patterns. I was reminded that kintsugi is not merely to repair the cracks and chips of a vessel, but to interpret the cracks and chips as "new scenery" and to design and repair the vessel while confronting and respecting its individuality.

Oribe developed and deepened the chado of Rikyu, and eventually dominated the tea world with the support of the power of the Tokugawa family. It is said that this was not because Oribe was fortunate enough to follow the trends of the times, but was because his strong personality, his wealth of knowledge learned from many cultural figures, and his skillful oratory made the times change.

した。

　織部は利休の茶の湯を発展・深化させ、やがて徳川家の力を背景に一世を風靡します。「へうげもの」「やきそこない（焼き損ない）」と言われた茶碗が茶席を賑わすという、ある意味常軌を逸した茶の湯が天下に認められたのです。これは、織部が幸運にも時代のトレンドに乗ったからではなく、彼の強烈な個性と多くの文化人から学んだ知識の豊富さ、加えて弁舌の巧さが時代を変えさせたのだ、と言われています。

　私はそれまで、職人は黙って手を動かすものだと思っていました。手を動かして熟達すれば、どこかで誰かが気づいて見てくれると思っていたのです。ところが、織部はプロデュース力とプレゼンテーション力を持った茶人であり武将でした。社会に「認められる」ためには、時代の到来を待っているだけではだめだ、ということを織部は私に気づかせてくれました。

　堺の一茶人だった千利休は、豊臣秀吉の側近にまで上り詰めましたが、秀吉との間柄が悪くなり、京都・大徳寺の金毛閣での一件が引き金となって、切腹を命ぜられます。加賀藩主・前田利家らは秀吉への助命嘆願を利休に勧めるものの、利休は自らの茶道理念に反するとして謝罪を拒否します。「頭を下げて守れるものもあれば、頭を下げるゆえに守れないものもある」とは利休の言葉です。1591年2月28日、利休の元に秀吉の使者がやってきて「切腹せよ」と伝えると、利休は「茶室に支度ができております」と応え、使者に生涯最後のお茶を点てた後、切腹しました。

　織部もまた、権力になびかない行動をとり続けた結果、謀反の疑いをかけられて切腹を命じられると、「かくなるうえは、さしたる申し開きなし」と一切の言い訳をせずにそれを受け入れます。両者とも死を賭してでも自分の信念を曲げず、最後まで己の追い求めた「美」の中に生きました。

　利休と織部について、陶芸家の加藤唐九郎氏（1897〜1985）は「利休は自然の中から美を見出した人だが、創り出した人ではない。織部は美を創り出した人で、芸術としての陶器は織部から始まっている」と述べています。なるほど、そうかもしれません。しかし、利休は茶道の中に侘びの心に繋がる「静けさ」を、織部は破調の美に繋がる「動き」を見出しました。

　茶道とは「一服の茶を差し上げる」、それだけのことながら、私はこの世の全てを含んだ「宇宙」が茶道にはあり、二人の茶人はそれに没頭し、それぞれのかたちで己を極めていったと思うのです。そして、茶碗を金継ぎ修復させていただきながら利休と織部のことを思うたびに私は、私の一生をかけても二人が見た「宇宙」の入口にも立てないと考えています。

I used to think that craftsmen were meant to be silent and to work with their hands; that if you moved your hands and became proficient, someone somewhere would take notice of you. However, Oribe was a tea master and warlord who had the ability to produce and present his creative ideas. Oribe made me realize that in order to be "recognized" by society, it is not enough to wait for the times to come.

Sen no Rikyu started his career as a tea master in Sakai, but rose to become a close aide of Toyotomi Hideyoshi, the most powerful man in Japan at the time. But his relationship with Hideyoshi deteriorated, and he was ordered to commit seppuku (ritual suicide) after an incident at the Kinmokaku main gate of Daitokuji Temple in Kyoto. Maeda Toshiie and others encouraged Rikyu to plead with Hideyoshi for his life, but Rikyu refused to apologize, saying it was against the philosophy of chado. On the 28th day of the 2nd month, 1591, a messenger from Hideyoshi came to Rikyu and told him to "commit seppuku." Rikyu responded, "I am ready in the tea room," and after making the last tea of his life for the messenger, he committed ritual suicide.

Oribe was falsely accused of treason and was ordered to commit ritual suicide, but he accepted the order, saying, "In that case, I make no excuses." Both Rikyu and Oribe did not bend to authority, even at the risk of death, and lived according to the aesthic they pursued to the end.

Speaking of Rikyu and Oribe, the late ceramic artist Tokuro Kato (1897–1985) said, "Rikyu was a man who found beauty in nature, but not a man who created it. Oribe is the one who created beauty, and pottery as an art form began with Oribe." Well, that may be true. However, I believe Rikyu found in chado the "stillness" that connects to the wabi spirit, and Oribe found the "movement" that connects to the beauty of the broken style.

Chado exists as a perfected expression of the concrete motivation "to offer a serving of tea," but I think that it encompasses a universe. These two tea masters immersed themselves in that view and mastered themselves in their own way. And every time I think about Rikyu and Oribe while I am restoring tea bowls with metal fittings, I think that even if I spent my whole life trying to get there, I would barely stand at the entrance of the universe they saw.

繕うこと、その精神性と文化、世界とのつながり | The World around Kintsugi Restoration

海外に渡った日本の漆芸
Japanese Lacquerware that has Gone Overseas

　日本の古典的な漆芸はいつ頃に海外へ運ばれたのか、ご存知でしょうか。

　15世紀から17世紀の大航海時代に日本を訪れた西欧の人々は、日本の漆器の美しさに魅了され、多くの品々を自国へと送りました。彼らの大きな関心を集めたという日本の漆器は西欧への貴重な輸出品となっていきますが、特に漆黒に金の蒔絵が際立っている作品は西欧貴族を魅了しました。蒔絵とは漆黒の表面に漆で絵を描き、乾かないうちに金や銀を蒔くという日本が生んだ工芸品で、これが「黄金の国ジパング」と呼ばれた由縁です。

　同じ頃、キリスト教の宣教師たちは、東洋での布教活動を積極的に進めており、彼らの注文を受けて、蒔絵によって教会で使う色々な道具もつくられています。フランシスコ・ザビエルの出身地であるスペインのナバーラには、精緻で美しい日本の漆器が数多く保存されています。

　また、かの有名な王妃マリー・アントワネッ

Do you know when classical Japanese lacquerware was first taken overseas? Western Europeans who visited Japan during the Age of Discovery, from the 15th to 17th centuries, were fascinated by the beauty of Japanese lacquerware and sent many items back to their countries. The Japanese lacquerware that attracted their attention became a valuable export to the West. Especially the works with outstanding gold maki-e on black lacquer attracted the Western aristocracy. Maki-e is a Japanese craft in which lacquer is painted on a black surface and gold or silver is sprinkled on the surface before it dries. The popularity of maki-e inspired Westerners to call Japan "Zipangu, the Land of Gold."

At the same time, Christian missionaries were actively promoting their missionary activities in the East, and various church items were made using maki-e in response to their orders. Many exquisite and beautiful Japanese lacquerware pieces are preserved in Navarra, Spain, the birthplace of Francisco de Xavier.

The famous Queen Marie Antoinette was fond of Japanese lacquerware. Her mother, Maria Theresa, the Empress of the Austrian Habsburgs, was an avid collector of lacquerware and even built a "lacquer room" in her palace in Vienna,

トも日本の漆器が大好きでした。もともと母親であるオーストリアのハプスブルク家の女帝マリア・テレジアが漆器の熱心なコレクターで「私は、ダイヤモンドより漆器よ」と言って、ウィーンの宮殿に「漆の間」をつくったほどでした。母の没後、マリー・ア

saying, "I prefer lacquerware to diamonds." After her mother's death, Marie Antoinette inherited as many as fifty pieces of lacquerware and continued to buy more. Her collection is said to be the largest in Western Europe in terms of both quality and quantity.

People in the West tried to reproduce expensive

ントワネットは50点もの漆器を相続し、その後も買い足していきました。そのコレクションは、西欧で質・量ともに随一と言われています。

　西欧の人々は高価な輸入品である日本の漆器を自分たちで再現しようと、後に「ジャパニング」と呼ばれる塗装工法を生み出しました。身近にある材料で「漆黒」を創造できないか研究を重ね、模倣品ながら高い水準のものをつくり上げました。

　元来、漆が生育しないヨーロッパでは、樹脂やオイルに黒色の粉末を混ぜた塗料を漆の代用としました。本物のクオリティーには及ばないものの、徐々に技術を向上させて、やがて「ジャパニング」はひとつの手法として定着します。例えば、ピアノの黒い色はジャパニングによるもので、もともとは木目調塗装が一般的でしたが、ジャパニングが普及してから黒く塗られるようになったのです。

　長い間西欧で珍重されてきた漆器は、修復を繰り返しながら承継されてきたものの、伝統的な漆芸工法が知られていないことから、行き届いた手入れが行われない状況でもありました。近年、西欧では日本の漆芸修復の研究が進み、金継ぎも知られるようになり、傷んだ箇所や破損した箇所を自然素材のみで直す手法が注目されています。

imported Japanese lacquerware by themselves, and developed a coating method called "Japanning." They researched to see if it was possible to create a "jet-black" finish using materials that were readily available, and although imitations, the resulting works were made to a high standard.

In Europe, where the lacquer tree does not grow, black powdered paint mixed with resin or oil was used as a substitute for lacquer. Although it could not match the quality of the real thing, the technique was gradually improved and eventually "Japanning" became established as a method. For example, the black color of pianos is due to Japanning. Originally, wood grain paint was common, but after Japanning became widespread, pianos were painted black.

Lacquerware has been prized in the West for a long time, and while it has been repeatedly restored, it has not been well cared for due to the lack of knowledge of traditional lacquerware techniques. In recent years, however, research on the restoration of Japanese lacquerware has progressed in the West. The processes of kintsugi have also become well known, attracting attention as a method of repairing damaged or broken parts using only natural materials.

繕うこと、その精神性と文化、世界とのつながり　｜　The World around Kintsugi Restoration

海外からみた繕い
Kintsugi as Seen from Overseas

　ここ数年で「金継ぎ」は「Kintsugi」という英単語で国際的に認識され、世界中でワークショップの開催や多くの関連書が出版されるようになりました。私自身も2020年にBBC（イギリスの放送会社）で10分ほどのドキュメンタリー特集を組んで紹介してもらいましたが、その再生回数は50万回を超え、今も増え続けています。その影響か、私のFacebookには世界中の色々な方からアクセスをいただいています。

　また、2020年に惜しくも亡くなったデザイナーの故高田賢三氏が、生前に立ち上げたラグジュアリーホームウエア＆ライフスタイルブランド「K3」は、家具や陶芸品、絨毯、オブジェ、リネン、テキスタイルなどを展開していますが、陶芸品には金継ぎ技法を用いるなど日本の伝統的な要素を取り込んだコレクションもあるようです。

　さらに、イタリアのジュエリーブランド「ポメラート」が金継ぎをあしらったデザインリングを発表しています。アメリカでは2019年公開の映画「スター・ウォーズ/スカイウォーカーの夜明け」で、主人公のカイロ・レンのマスクが金継ぎされていたことが話題になりました。また同国では「Kintsugi」とい

In the past few years, the Japanese word "kintsugi" has come to be recognized internationally, workshops have been held all over the world, and many related books have been published. In 2020, the BBC (British Broadcasting Company) made a feature documentary on kintsugi. It has been viewed more than 500,000 times, and this number is still increasing. Perhaps because of this, my Facebook page is being visited by people from all over the world.

"K3," a luxury homeware and lifestyle brand launched by the late designer Kenzo Takada, who sadly passed away in 2020, offers furniture, ceramics, carpets, objects, linens, and textiles. Some collections of K3 incorporate traditional Japanese elements, such as the use of kintsugi in ceramics.

In addition, the Italian jewelry brand Pomellato has released a design ring featuring kintsugi. In the U.S., the main character Kylo Ren in the movie Rise of Skywalker treasures a mended mask which features kintsugi. In the U.S., There is also an active Physical Therapy & Wellness organization named "Kintsugi." NHK (Japan Broadcasting Corporation) broadcasted that a romantic film titled "Kintsugi" was produced and released in the spring of 2021 in the Philippines.President Andrew Parsons of the International Paralympic Committee, In his speech at the closing ceremony of the Tokyo 2020 Paralympic Games which were postponed a year due to the coronavirus crisis, talked of Japan's "philosophy called kintsugi," saying that

う名前のPhysical Therapy & Wellness（理学療法）の団体が活発に活動しています。フィリピンでは「Kintsugi」というタイトルの恋愛映画が制作され、2021年春に公開されたと、以前NHKで紹介されていました。

そして、国際パラリンピック委員会のアンドリュー・パーソンズ会長は、コロナ禍で1年延期となった東京2020パラリンピック閉会式のスピーチで、「金継ぎの精神性」について「誰もが持つ不完全さを受け入れ、隠すのではなく大事にしようという考え方です」と紹介し、その上で「スポーツの祭典の間、私たちは違いを認め、多様性の調和を見せました。私たちの旅をここで終わらせてはいけません。今日は閉会式というよりも、すべての人が共生できる未来への始まりと捉えてください」と結びました。

金継ぎで表現された日本人の精神性が世界中に知られ、受け入れられているのは素晴らしいことです。その一方で、簡易的なものではなく、江戸時代の職人が完成させた伝統的な金継ぎと漆芸の技法を世界に正しく伝えることが必要であると思うようになりました。古典的な技法の裏にある漆と日本人との共生の歴史や、自然素材を用いた修復にまつわる職人の古来の知恵についての情報発信は、日本の伝統文化と日本人の精神性を海外の方に知ってもらうためには、とても大事なことだと思うのです。

"it means to embrace the imperfections we all have; to not hide them away, but to celebrate them." He followed this up by saying, "During our carnival of sports, we have celebrated difference, exhibited the best of humanity, and showed unity in diversity. However our journey cannot end here. Tonight [is] not like a closing ceremony, but an opening to a bright and inclusive future."

It is wonderful that the spirituality of the Japanese people expressed through kintsugi is known and accepted all over the world. On the other hand, I have come to believe that it is necessary to properly convey to the world the traditional techniques of kintsugi and lacquerware, which were perfected by the extraordinary craftsmen of the Edo period (1603–1868). A merely symbolic and simplified version of the tradition will not suffice. I think it is important to provide concrete and detailed information about the history of the symbiosis between lacquer and the Japanese people. Details of the classical techniques and applied wisdom of craftsmen performing restoration using only natural materials are fundamental to an understanding of Japan's traditional culture and the spirituality of the Japanese people.

海外からみた繕い | Kintsugi as Seen from Overseas

国連事務総長のスピーチ
Speech by the Secretary-General of the United Nations

　国際連合（国連）は9月21日を非暴力と停戦を呼びかける「国際平和デー」と定め、毎年この前後に日本で平和活動に取り組んだ愛媛県の中川千代治氏から1954年に贈られた「平和の鐘」を鳴らす式典を行っています。

　2020年9月18日のNHKのニュースで、「国際平和デー」に合わせてニューヨークの国連本部で行われた式典でのアントニオ・グテーレス事務総長のスピーチが紹介されました。

　ニュースによれば、事務総長は式典で「新型コロナウイルスは至るところで平和を脅かし、とりわけ紛争下にいる人々にとてつもない脅威をもたらしている」と述べ、人々に必要な支援を届けるためにも、紛争地での戦闘を停止するよう呼びかけたということです。

　さらに、「平和の鐘」が世界中のコイン（金貨）を溶かして造られたことをふまえ、壊れた陶磁器を修復する日本の金継ぎに触れて「金継ぎは金と漆を使って壊れた陶磁器をより強く、より美しくする。破壊された世界にこの精神を届けよう」と述べて、平和への想いを訴えました。

　コロナ禍の現在、金継ぎの精神性を世界平和に繋げて、国連の事務総長が紹介してくれたことに、私は感銘を受けました。

The UN (United Nations) has designated September 21 as the "International Day of Peace," a call for universal non-violence and ceasefire. Every year around this date, a ceremony is held to ring the "Peace Bell," which was presented in 1954, by Chiyoji Nakagawa of Ehime Prefecture, a peace activist in Japan at the time.

On September 18, 2020, NHK news introduced Secretary-General Antonio Guterres' speech in the ceremony held at the UN Headquarters in New York on the occasion of the International Day of Peace.

According to the news report, Guterres said that "the new coronavirus threatens peace everywhere and poses a tremendous threat, especially to people in conflict," and called for a halt to fighting in conflict zones so that people can get the help they need.

The Secretary-General also said, "Japanese culture has a deep appreciation for natural imperfections and flaws. This is reflected in the art of kintsugi—putting broken pieces of pottery together with golden lacquer to create a stronger, more beautiful whole. The result is a piece that is not 'good as new', but 'better than new.' As we mark the International Day of Peace, let's apply this principle to our fractured world."

I was impressed that the Secretary-General of the United Nations introduced the spirituality of kintsugi, linking it to world peace in this time of the pandemic disaster.

海外からみた繕い｜出会い 1

新しい景色、新しい一日
とあるスイス人の訪問

「この茶碗を割ってくれませんか？ 私と私の友のために」

2018年の夏、ようやく梅雨が明けて日差しが強くなってきたある日の午後、工房を訪ねてきた長身のスイス人の男性は、桐箱の中から大事そうに茶碗を差し出すと、流暢な日本語で私に話しかけてきました。

茶碗は見事な京焼で、彼には白釉を使った器の表面が以前働いていた中東の砂漠に見えるようで、言われてみると白い釉薬のうねりは砂丘を思わせました。その茶碗で点てる抹茶は緑のオアシスのようです、と彼は私に言いました。

スイス生まれのルカはアラブ首長国連邦ドバイにある勤務先から2013年の秋に日本に出向し、神戸でエンジニアとして働いていました。彼は「壊れ」から「新しい景色」をつくる金継ぎ修復の精神性に共感して私の教室に入会してくれましたが、実は彼には金継ぎを学びたいもう一つの理由がありました。

それは、「ドバイの病院でがん闘病中の親友に、自ら直した器をプレゼントすることで、再生と復活を願って励ましたい」というものでした。

「マスター清川、この茶碗を割ってくれませんか？ 私と私の友のために」

蟬時雨が聞こえてくる暑い夏の昼下がり、穏やかな口調ながら懸命に話す姿を見て、私はルカに言いました。

「それならば一緒に壊して、一緒に繕いましょう。君の友に再生した器の"新しい景色"を見せてあげるために」

ルカと私は一緒に茶碗を割り、完品だった器を10ピースほどの破片にしました。その後、ルカは2週間に一度、仕事の合間に京都へ来て、黙々と茶碗を直し、その全ての過程を写真と文章に残していました。

ルカは多くを語りませんでしたが、修復する彼の後ろ姿は不思議な静けさに満ちていました。後に聞いたところ、ルカは壊れた器と向き合いながら親友のことを思い、器が修復されていくごとに病気が良くなることを信じて、神に祈りを捧げていたそうです。

半年後、ルカと私は元のかたちに戻った茶碗に金を蒔きました。

「金は邪悪なものを寄せつけない力があります。この茶碗に込められた君の願いが彼の力になりますように」

ルカは茶碗を繋ぐ金の輝きを砂漠の日の出に見立て、そこに生まれた新しい景色を「日新中砂漠（New Day in the Desert）」と名付け、私は心を込めてその名を箱書しました。

数日後、茶碗とその修復の過程を記したノートを持って、ルカはドバイ行きの飛行機に乗り闘病中の親友の元へ向かいました。

たとえどんな逆境に置かれても、それを足がかりにして「新しい一日」が始まることを伝えるために。

Kintsugi as Seen from Overseas | Encounter 1

A New View and a New Start
Receiving a visitor from Switzerland

"Master Kiyokawa, will you please break this tea bowl for me and my friend?"

One afternoon in the early summer of 2018, when the rainy season had finally ended and the sun was shining brightly, a tall swiss man came to visit me at my studio and, speaking fluent Japanese, he started talking to me as he carefully negotiated a tea bowl from its paulownia box.

The bowl, with its white glaze, looked to him like the deserts of the Middle East where he used to work, he said. The undulations of the white glaze were like sand dunes. He told me that when matcha was served in the bowl, it was like the green of an oasis in the desert.

Swiss-born Luka had lived in the Middle East for many years, where he worked as an engineer. He was transferred to Kobe in the fall of 2013 from Dubai, United Arab Emirates, He had heard about kintsugi restoration and the motivation to create "new scenery" from something broken, and the philosophy resonated with him. He signed up for my kintsugi class, but actually he had a deeper reason for wanting to restore his favorite tea bowl.

His best friend had been diagnosed with cancer, and was battling the disease in a hospital in Dubai. Luka wanted to encourage his friend by giving him a tea bowl that had once been broken, but was restored, its spirit intact.

On that hot summer afternoon, with the cicadas' clamor in the air, I saw how intently Luka was speaking, so I said to him, "Let's break this bowl together and also mend it together, so that your friend can see the 'new view' of the rebuilt vessel."

Luka agreed, and we broke the tea bowl together. It shattered into about ten pieces. Beginning that day, Luka managed his work schedule to find time to come to my studio in Kyoto every two weeks. He worked silently and restored the bowl bit by bit, while documenting the entire process with photos and texts.

He did not say much, but the back of his head as he restored the tea bowl had a strange calmness about it. I was later told that Luka was actively thinking about his best friend as he contemplated the broken vessel, and was giving thanks to God, believing that his friend's illness would get better as the vessel was repaired.

Six months later, Luka and I sowed gold on the bowl, which had been restored to its original shape.

Gold has the power to keep evil at bay, I thought, imagining the face of Luka's friend looking with wonder and joy at the restored tea bowl. May the effort of this restoration and our good wishes really help you, I thought.

Luka likened the glow of the gold on the tea bowl to the sunrise in the desert, and named the new landscape that emerged, "New Day in the Desert." I put my heart into it when I inscribed this name on the bowl's box.

Luka took the bowl and his notebook describing the restoration process to his friend in Dubai. He hoped to convey to his friend a fundamental principle of kintsugi as well as an auspicious perspective on life: no matter what the situation, taking a deliberate step forward can give us a new view, and a new start.

海外からみた繕い｜出会い 2

想いをつなぐ
とあるスペイン人の訪問

「僕と幼馴染の彼はとても仲が良くて、僕が郷里を離れる時、彼は一番大事にしていた戦士のフィギュアを僕にくれたのです。ずっと大切にしていたのに、突然首が取れてしまいました。マスター清川、フィギュアの首を二度と取れないように金継ぎしてもらえませんか？」

メディア取材を通じて知り合ったスペイン人の青年ダニエルは、日本の大学院で経営学を勉強している学生です。彼は独自に金継ぎ修復のことを調べていたようで、郷里のスペインにいる幼馴染からもらった樹脂製のフィギュアの取れてしまった首を何とか元に戻したいと思い、メディアのスタッフと一緒に私を訪ねてくれたのでした。

ダニエルは私と一緒に修復を行うことを希望し、メディアはその様子を収録することでドキュメンタリーを制作することになっていました。

ダニエルの依頼を聞いた時、私の中で、日本古来の漆で化学素材をどこまで修復できるだろうか、という興味が出てきました。私は漆で陶磁器やガラスの修復を行ったことはありますが、樹脂などの化学素材の修復は初めてだったので、今回の依頼は漆芸修復の可能性を知る良い機会だと思ったのです。化学素材の修復を自然素材のみで試みるという、私の挑戦でした。

修復を始める前、私はダニエルに言いました。

「私は君の大切なフィギュアを、君の幼馴染のことを心に浮かべて修復するよ。だって私は彼に会うことはおそらく叶わないからね。だから君も彼と過ごした日々を大事に思い出しながら直してほしい」

ダニエルは私の話を聞くと涙ぐんで、横にいたスタッフに撮影の一時中断を頼み、実は幼馴染はもうこの世にいないことを話してくれました。

「とても仲が良くて、僕が両親の仕事の都合で郷里を離れる時、彼は一番大事にしていた戦士のフィギュアを分身として、僕にくれたのです。だけど、僕は彼に最後のお別れを言えなかった。それがずっと心残りなのです」

彼は、胸の奥にしまっていた幼馴染との思い出を打ち明けてくれました。家の近くにある川に一緒に魚釣りに行ったこと、学校帰りに必ず立ち寄った森の中の小屋のこと、ダニエルと幼馴染は兄弟のようにいつも一緒で、そして二人とも自然の中で遊ぶことが好きだったこと……。

「マスター清川、このフィギュアを自然素材だけで直してほしいのです。だって、友達は自然が大好きだったから」

私はフィギアの折れた断面を調べて、表具師（ひょうぐし）が用いる「喰い裂き（くいさき）」の技法を応用して修復を行うことにしました。漆と米粉（こめこ）と和紙を混ぜ合わせて作った「のり漆」でフィギュアの首と胴を接着し、さらに和紙を巻いて接着部分を補強

Kintsugi as Seen from Overseas | Encounter 2

Passing Memories on to the Future
Receiving a visitor from Spain

"We were very close, and when I left my hometown, he gave me his most prized statuette of a warrior. I cherished it for a long time, but one day suddenly its head broke off. Master Kiyokawa, could I ask you to fix it with kintsugi so that the head it will always remain intact?

Daniel, a young Spanish man whom I met through a media interview, was studying business administration at a graduate school in Japan. Unrelated to his university studies, however, and motivated by passionate personal reasons, he was also conducting research on kintsugi restoration. He came to me with a media staff member to restore the statuette which had broken at the neck. It was given to him by a dear childhood friend in his hometown in Spain.

I had restored ceramics and glass, but this was to be my first experience with resin and other chemical materials. When I heard about Daniel's request, I became curious about the extent to which modern materials could be restored with the ancient techniques of Japanese lacquering. The future will see an ever wider range of requests for restoration, I thought, and recognized with gratitude that Daniel's request would present a good opportunity to explore the actual possibilities of using lacquer to restoreobjects.

Daniel was to work with me on the restoration, and the media organization was going to make a documentary recording the process.

Before we got started, I said to Daniel, "I think this figure is the real reason for doing this project. I'm going to restore this figure in honor of your childhood friend, whom I will probably never meet. I want you to work on the restoration keeping your friend in mind, as well."

When Daniel heard this, he broke down in tears, asked the crew beside him to to pause the filming and revealed that his childhood friend was actually no longer alive.

"We were very close, and when it was time for me to move away because of my parents' work, my friend gave me this, his prized warrior, as a kind of embodiment of him and token of our friendship. Years later I couldn't make it back to say final farewells to my friend before illness took his life. I've always regretted that."

He shared with me memories of his friend that he had been keeping in the back of his mind. They used to go fishing together at a nearby river, and they always stopped by a cabin in the forest when they played together after school. Daniel and his friend were like brothers, always together, and they both loved to play in nature.

"Master Kiyokawa, I want you to fix this figure using only natural materials, because my friend loved and respected nature very much."

I inspected the broken cross-section of the statuette and decided to repair it by applying a technique used by traditional paperers. I would first affix the head to the body with nori-urushi made of lacquer, rice powder, and Japanese paper, and then wrap Japanese paper around the glued parts to reinforce them. Next I would apply sabi-urushi, a mixture of raw lacquer

した後、砥の粉（山の土）と漆を混ぜて作った「錆漆」をそこに載せていきます。錆漆が硬化したら鑢で研いで表面を整え、黒漆と色漆で塗りを行い、最後に接着部分と胴体に金を蒔いて、修復したフィギアに新しい命を与えようと考えました。

　最初、私の気持ちは、化学素材の修復に対する自然素材の可能性を探ることに向いていました。しかし、ダニエルの話を聞いてから、フィギュア修復を通して彼の「幼馴染への想い」を未来に繋ぐことに切り替わりました。

　ダニエルは将来、自分の子どもにフィギュアを見せて、幼馴染との思い出を話して聞かせるでしょう。父の話を聞いた子どもは、きっとフィギュアを大事に手元に置いて過ごし、やがてそれは、思い出話と共にダニエルの孫に託されるのです。そうやって、人の想いは時を超えて繋がっていくのだと思います。

　ダニエルと私はフィギュアの修復中、互いの気持ちを同化させて、早世した幼馴染のことを考えました。フィギュアの修復が仕上げの段階に入り、最後に首から胴にかけて金を蒔いた後、それは新たな命を得て、彼の手に在りました。ダニエルはその時、私にこう言いました。

　「新しい景色が生まれたことによって、今友達が私のところに来てくれたように感じます。マスター清川、僕に特別な時間をプレゼントしてくれてありがとう」

and powdered clay. Once this layer hardened, I would sand it down, then apply black and colored lacquer, and finally sprinkle gold on the glued parts and the body.

At first, my mind was focused on exploring the possibilities of natural materials for restoring chemical materials. However, after listening to Daniel's story, my focus changed; my thought was to connect his love for his childhood friend to the future through the restoration of this symbolic figure.

Daniel would show the statuette to his children and tell them about his memories of his childhood friend. They will listen to their father's story and keep the statuette, and eventually it will be passed on to Daniel's ggrandchildren, along with their grandfather's story. In this way, I believe that people's memories are passed on across time.

While Daniel and I were restoring the statuette, despite the language barrier we assimilated a great deal of each other's feelings. We thought together, and in our own ways, about his childhood friend.

Once the restoration of the statuette was units firuishing stage and the final gold was applied to the neck and body, it took on a new life in his hands. Daniel said to me, "My statuette has been resurrected and has received a new life. I feel that my friend is here too, enjoying this moment with me. Master Kiyokawa, thank you for giving me this precious experience."

海外からみた繕い ｜ 出会い 3

先端と伝統の融合
イタリアの会社の訪問

　2年ほど前、イタリアのミラノに本社があるゴッピオン社（Goppion S.p.A.）の社長とそのご子息、専属デザイナーの3人が、私の工房を訪問してくれました。ゴッピオン社は、美術館のディスプレイケースの設計・制作をしている会社で、その高度な技術と洗練されたデザインから、フランスのルーブル美術館をはじめとする世界の名だたる美術館のコレクションの展示ケースを引き受けています。

　彼らの訪問の目的は、最先端の保管技術に自然素材を用いた昔ながらの技法を応用することで、美術品をより良く管理できないか、ヒントを見つけることでした。私はひと通り漆芸修復の工程を説明し、彼らに金継ぎの一日体験をしてもらいました。

　すると、ゴッピオン社の社長が「なんだ、我々が研究開発しようとしている技法とその答えは全部ここにあるじゃないか」と言ったのです。彼らの驚嘆した姿を見て、私は日本の伝統技法を外国の方に紹介できたことを嬉しく思うのと同時に、45年間、私が毎日のように行ってきた仕事が、国を越えて認められることの価値を知りました。今、風前の灯火である日本の古典的職人技術が海外でも注目される中、その技術承継のあるべき姿を、私は模索しています。

Kintsugi as Seen from Oversea ｜ Encounter 3

Fusion of Advanced Technology and Traditional Techniques
Visited by an Italian company

About two years ago, the president of Goppion S.p.A., headquartered in Milan, Italy, visited my studio along with his son and a head designer of his company. Goppion S.p.A. is a company that designs and produces display cases for museums. Because of their advanced technology and sophisticated designs, they have been commissioned to produce display cases for the collections of the Louvre and other world-famous museums.

The purpose of their visit was to find out how art can be better stored by applying the traditional way using only natural materials to state-of-the-art storage technology. I briefly explained the process of lacquer art restoration and gave them a one-day experience of kintsugi.

The president of Goppion said to me, "Why, all the techniques and answers we have been trying to research and develop over the years are right here!" Seeing their amazement made me happy. I felt gratified to be able to introduce Japanese traditional techniques to people from overseas, and at the same time have the value of my daily work, which I have been doing every day for 45 years, recognized beyond national borders. Now, as Japan's classical craftsmen's techniques are attracting attention overseas, I am searching for the best way to pass on these techniques.

海外からみた繕い ｜ 出会い 4

アンブレイカブル　Unbreakable
とあるイタリア人の訪問

　2017年に私が日本で金継ぎ修復を教えたイタリア人のキアラは、もともとイタリアの古美術品の修復師でしたが、日本の金継ぎ修復の技術と考え方に大きな魅力を感じて、はるばるイタリアから私を訪ねてくれました。

　彼女はイタリアと日本の修復に対する考え方が、全く異なることに気づいていました。イタリアの修復は「壊れたこと」を無かったことにするべく、壊れた部分が全く分からないように隠して修復しようとしますが、日本は「壊れたこと」をその物が持っている宿命として受け入れて、修復後の姿に「新たな景色」を与えることを考え、そこに価値を見出そうとします。つまり、「壊れ」を隠さず生かして、修復品に新たな命を与えるのです。

　また、イタリアではしばしば修復に合成接着剤を使いますが、日本では自然素材のみで行います。キアラは、私の工房で数日を過ごした後、母国に帰って私の教えに沿った金継ぎ教室を開催し、伝統的な日本の金継ぎ修復を広く巷間に紹介してくれました。

　2019年、イタリアのある自動車メーカーがキアラの活動に注目し、「金継ぎ」の精神を反映したコマーシャルフィルムを制作してくれました。この自動車メーカーは「東京2020パラリンピック」の公式スポンサーで、支援するパラリンピックの選手の方々の身体と補助具の繋がりを金継ぎになぞらえ、映像をつくり上げたのです。

　パラリンピックに出場する全ての選手は、生まれながらの障害や予期せぬ事故に遭遇するなど、様々な事情で身体に障害を抱えています。時には自分の障害を受け入れることができず、生きる目標を見失ってしまったこともあったかと思います。けれども、選手たちは己の宿命と向き合い、それを受け入れることを決意し、人生を諦めませんでした。多くの医療従事者のサポートを得て、新しい手足や補助具を手にしてからは、厳しいトレーニングに耐えてそれを使いこなし、障害の向こうに「新たな景色」を見出して、前向きに歩んでこられました。

　障害のある方と補助具を繋ぐのは、本人の強い意志と周りの大きなサポートです。金、銀、銅のメダルは、割れ欠けした器に装飾する金蒔きのような、選手のたゆまぬ努力への「美しい装飾」です。パラリンピックの選手とその人生は、どんなことがあっても決して壊れることはない、正に「アンブレイカブル（Unbreakable）」なものなのです。

Kintsugi as Seen from Overseas | Encounter 4

Unbreakable
Receiving a visitor from Italy

Chiara, an Italian lady who attended my kintsugi restoration classes in Japan in 2017, was originally an antique restorer. She came all the way from Italy to Japan to visit me because she was fascinated by the methods and concepts of kintsugi restoration.

She proposed that the Italian and Japanese approaches to restoration were different from the very start. In Italy, restoration is done in principle to erase any apparent brokenness, so that it is not perceptible at all. In Japan, however, the brokenness is accepted as the fate of the object, and openly displayed. The restoration, far from an erasure, is rather a kind of organic outgrowth of that brokenness. Rather than being erased, the scars of breakage are interpreted as the "new scenery" of the vessel, born of happenstances unique to it and deepening its appeal and value.

Also in Italy, synthetic adhesives are often used for restoration, but in Japan, restoration is done using only natural materials. Chiara spent a few days in my workshop and then went back to her home country to hold a kintsugi class in accordance with my teachings, introducing the methods of traditional Japanese kintsugi restoration to the local public.

In 2019, a car manufacturer in Italy took notice of Chiara's activities and made a commercial film reflecting the principles of kintsugi. This car manufacturer is an official sponsor of the 2020 Tokyo Paralympics, and in their film they connected the Paralympic athletes they support with the spirit of kintsugi.

All Paralympic athletes have physical disabilities due to various reasons such as birth defects or unexpected accidents. In the past, they may have been unable to accept the fact of their disabilities, and may even have lost sight of their purpose in life. However, these athletes decided to face their circumstances, accept them, and move forward in their lives. After receiving the support of many medical professionals, they have endured rigorous training and been able to explore new vistas beyond their disabilities.

Connecting people with disabilities with the care they need comes about not just from the strong intention to help, but from the actual support of engaged individuals. The gold, silver, and bronze medals are a beautiful tribute to the tireless efforts of the athletes, and to the perseverance of all those who support them to move forward. These medals are not unlike the gold sown on broken vessels. The lives of the Paralympic athletes are truly "unbreakable." The accidents of history can never diminish them, but only add luster to their shine.

繕うこと、その精神性と文化、世界とのつながり | The World around Kintsugi Restoration

琵琶法師との出会い

A Request for Biwa Restoration from Master Musician Kakuyu Sekikawa

　関川鶴祐さんは臨済宗建長寺派の僧籍であり、日本を代表する薩摩琵琶の奏手でもあります。

　ある時、師匠から譲り受けた150年ほど前の大事な琵琶を持って、修復のために工房に来てくださいました。琵琶は桑の木を主材とし、絃はその葉を食べる蚕がつくる絹でできています。漆で化粧と保護が琵琶全体に行われ、漆黒に施された蒔絵装飾は「宇宙」を表現しているといいます。薩摩琵琶は演奏時、大きな黄楊の木の撥で本体の胴と絃を激しく叩くので、胴は傷んで漆と蒔絵が剝がれており、長年の使用で汚れと油が漆の上に張りついて、全体が曇っていました。

　私は、修復を引き受けるにあたり条件をつけました。

　「関川さんと私とで一緒に作業をしましょう。この琵琶の寿命は、私たちの寿命より遥かに永く、次に託す方にも修復の仕方を理解し繋げていただくために一緒に取り組みましょう。お住いの奈良から幾度も足を

Mr. Kakuyu Sekikawa is both a Buddhist priest and also one of the most famous Satsuma biwa players in Japan. He is renowned throughout Japan as one of the most remarkable living masters of the Satsuma biwa musical lineage.

One day, he came to my workshop to consult with me about restoring his biwa, which was made about 150 years ago. This was his master's instrument, handed down to him by his master when he was young, and he treasured it like nothing else. The body of the biwa was mulberry wood, and the strings are made from silk produced by silkworms that feed on mulberry leaves. The instrument body was decorated with traditional gold lacquer maki-e in a swirling, luminous design representing the cosmos. The body of the instrument had significant damage. The lacquer and maki-e had chipped and peeled away after years of being struck strongly with the large boxwood plectrum. Grime and oil had accumulated on the lacquer over the years, making the whole body cloudy and dull.

I agreed to take on the restoration, but made one condition, which was that Master Sekikawa and I do the restoration work together. The life of this biwa is much longer than ours, I reasoned, and asked if he would collaborate with me so that he could teach the next custodian of the instrument how to care for it

Chapter 3 89
章

琵琶法師との出会い | A Request for Biwa Restoration from Master Musician Kakuyu Sekikawa

運んでいただくことになりますが」とお願いをしました。

「是非お願いしたいです」

「はい、よろこんで」

それから半年、関川さんは月に2回ほど、私の工房に来てくれています。

私たちはまず、琵琶に塗られた黒漆を覆（おお）っている積年の汚れの被膜を、呂色粉（ろいろこ）（深みのある艶（つや）に仕上げる漆磨き専用の粉）を用いて指先で丁寧に研磨して剥（けんま）がして、150年前の漆の輝きを取り戻すようにしました。

その後、私は友人の京指物師（きょうさしものし）の工房に琵琶を持ち込み、琵琶の棹（さお）上部に固定された板状のフレット（柱（ちゅう）ともいう）の作り替えを依頼しました。フレットを新調することで琵琶の絃は棹にバランス良く張られて、奏者は深い音色を出せるようになります。

また、激しい演奏により縦に割れてしまった黄楊の撥の修理を頼みました。指物師は、一枚木の撥の割れた断面にダボ板（木材同士を繋ぎ合わせる際に使用する小さな板、突起のこと。繋ぎ合わせたい木材の双方にダボ板と同じ厚さの溝（みぞ）をあけ、それぞれの溝にダボ板を差し込み合体させることでぴったりと繋ぐことが可能）を入れて補

properly. Even though it would require many trips from Nara, he heartily agreed.

For the next half year, the Master Sekikawa came to my workshop about twice a month.

We started by carefully polishing the black lacquer on the biwa with roiro powder to remove the film of grime that had accumulated over the years, so that the biwa could regain its original lacquer shine.

After that, I entrusted the biwa to the workshop of one of the best sashimono woodwork craftsmen in Kyoto and asked him to rebuild the instrument's frets. With new frets, the strings of the biwa would be stretched in a balanced manner, and the instrument would produce a deeper and more resonant tone.

I also asked him to repair the large wooden plectrum that had cracked vertically due to decades of intense playing. The sashimono craftsman put dowels into the broken cross section of the single piece of wood to both repair and reinforce it, and repaired it so that it could withstand even the player's most powerful performance.

I was told by Master Sekikawa that it would be impossible today to find a boxwood tree large enough to make a plectrum of the size that he uses.

He had asked around at instrument repair and woodworking shops to repair the plectrum, but none of them would take the job because no one there had the advanced skills to strengthen

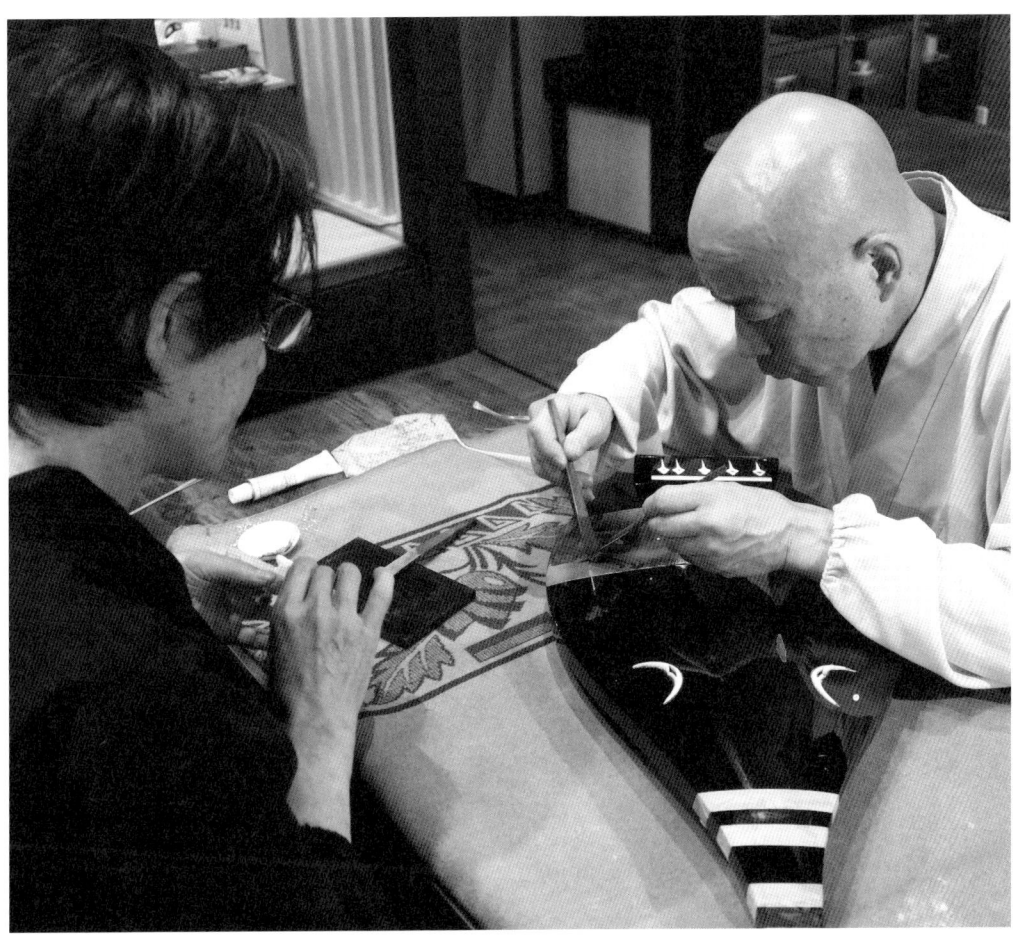

強し、奏者の力強い演奏に耐えられるように修復してくれました。

　私は関川さんから「現在、私の持つ撥が作れるだけの黄楊の大木を見つけることは到底できないのです」と聞いていました。

　関川さんは撥の修理を楽器店や木工所に頼みましたが、薄い撥に強度をつけて繋げる高い技術を誰一人として持っておらず、どこも引き受けてくれなかったそうです。彼

and connect a thin plectrum. He wondered at the now beautifully restored plectrum, turning it over in his hands and saying over and over again that he could not believe it was fixed.

A little about the sashimono craftsman who repaired the biwa and the plectrum. He is 80 years old and has no successor. The first thing that struck me when I entered his workshop was the number of tools he had, and the meticulous care that he took of them. He had about 30 planes alone. The quality of a

琵琶法師との出会い | A Request for Biwa Restoration from Master Musician Kakuyu Sekikawa

は修復された撥を手に持って、「直ったことが信じられない」と何度も言っていました。

琵琶と撥を直してくれた指物師は御年80歳ですが、後継者はいません。

彼の工房には鉋だけで約30丁はありました。一流の職人は仕事場と道具をみれば、その技術の高さが分かります。手入れされた道具が整然と並んでいる仕事場はとても美しく、どんな作業にも素早く対応できるのです。私は、この道具たちと指物師が持つ技術と感性を受け継ぐ者がいないことに、口惜しさと寂しさを覚えました。

同時に、修理された撥に職人技術の凄みを見て、それが遠くない未来途絶えてしまう危機感を持たざるを得ませんでした。

指物師の修復を終えた琵琶は良い音を奏でるようになりましたが、これから関川さんと私は、胴体の剥がれた漆と蒔絵の修復を行います。この琵琶が、指物師と関川さんと私の想いを載せて何百年も演奏されるように、私は手を入れていきたいと思います。

「関川さんや琵琶とのご縁は、私と工房にとって宝物になることに違いない」。そんな風に思いつつ、お預かりしている琵琶との時間を大切にしています。

craftsman can be understood by his workshop. I think it is very beautiful to see a workshop where well-kept tools are arranged in a designated way.

The fact that there was nobody to inherit those tools and the skills that this sashimono craftsman possessed made me feel distressed and sad. Seeing the amazing craftsmanship that had gone into fixing the large plectrum, I couldn't help but feel a keen sense of urgency that such craftsmanship will probably cease to exist in the not-too-distant future.

Now that the biwa has been repaired by the sashimono craftsman, it sounds good again, but it is still up to Master Sekikawa and me to restore the urushi finish and maki-e decoration. I would like to do my work on restoring this biwa so that this instrument will be played for hundreds of years to come, carrying within it the heart that we poured into restoring it.

The time that I am spending with this biwa holds great significance for me. I think that the fortunate fate which has connected me and my workshop with Master Sekikawa and his biwa will surely become our treasure.

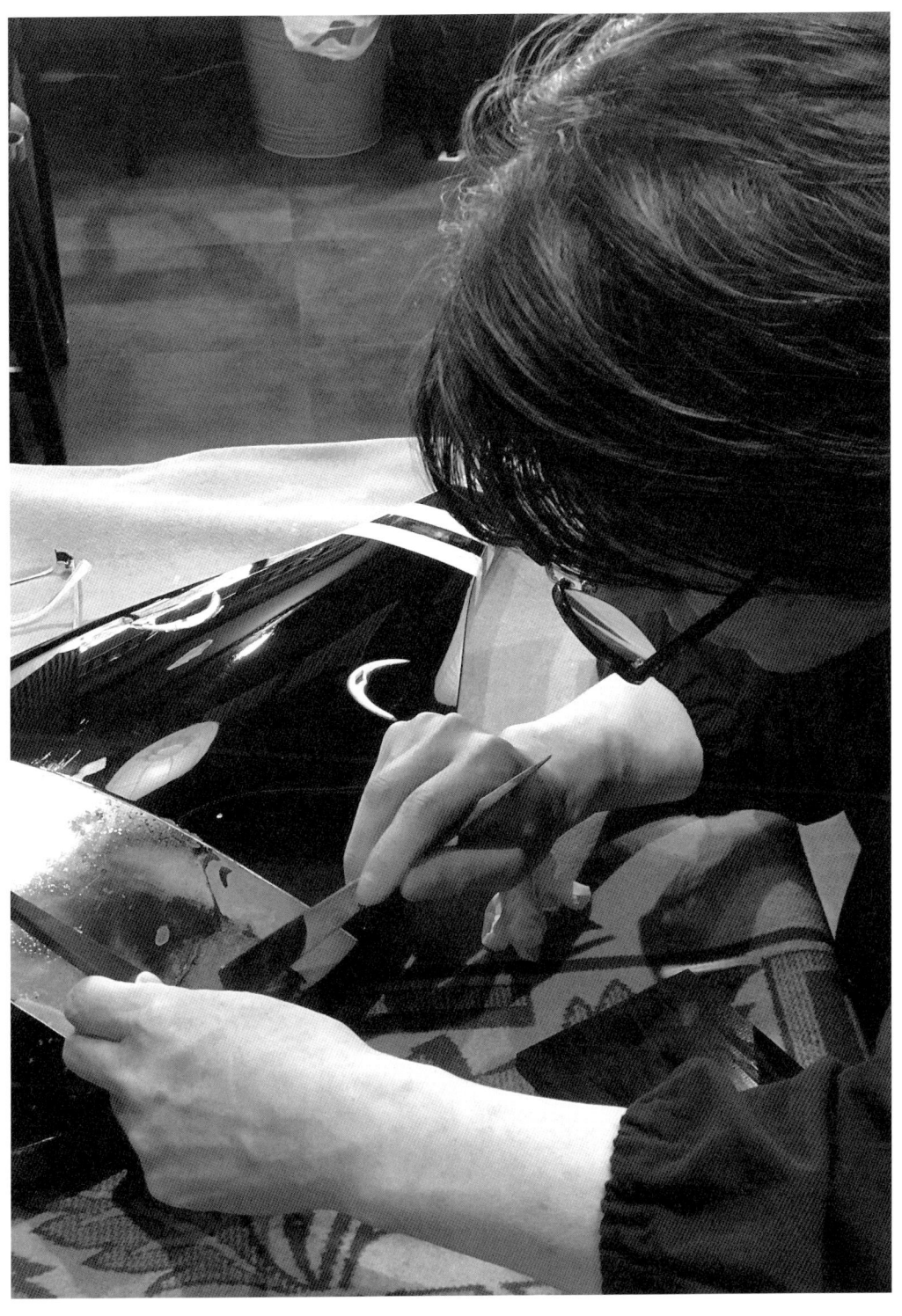

Chapter 3　93
章

お茶碗を直す
少年から頼まれた繕い

　今から数年前、神戸からあるご夫婦と二人の息子さんが工房を訪ねてくださいました。お子さんは、上の子がわんぱくな小学校2年生で、下の子は幼稚園生でした。

　二人は人気キャラクターがプリントされたお揃いのお茶碗を持っていて、とても気に入っていましたが、上の子は力加減ができず、大事なお茶碗を欠けさせてしまいました。彼はとても残念がり「何とか元に戻したい」ということで、工房に来てくれたのです。

　私は欠けた茶碗を手に持って、その子の前で修復価格の見積もりを行いました。私はどんな高価な器でも普段使いの食器であっても、破損の程度（欠け一か所でいくら、割れ一か所でいくらといった具合）で見積もります。彼のお茶碗の欠けはそれほど大きくなかったのですが、目立っていて、見積りの結果は1万5000円ほどになりました。

　私は彼に金継ぎ修復の工程と、完成までに要する日にちを説明し、「欠けて痛かったお茶碗へ、我慢したご褒美（ほうび）に最後に金を蒔く」という装飾を提案しました。

　最初は、「おそらく数百円くらいで簡単に修理できるだろう」と思っていた男の子は、私が見積りで加算していくたびに心配そうな顔になり、「合計1万5000円で」と話した時は本当にびっくりした顔をしていました。でも、私は彼の後ろでお母さんが「してやったり」といったお顔で微笑んでいるのを見逃しませんでした。

　男の子は自分のお年玉から修復代を払い、2か月後の修復完了後にご家族でお茶碗を引き取りにきてくれました。きれいに金継ぎされたお茶碗は、欠けてしまう前よりも美しく輝いていました。

　「ありがとう」

　「きれいに直しました。お茶碗はきっと喜んでいますよ」

　私は、わんぱくな男の子が両手でお茶碗を大事そうに持ったことに気づきました。そしてお母さんを見ると、見積りの時と同じように息子を見てニッコリされていました。

　しばらくして、ご両親からご丁寧なお礼状をいただきました。そこには、その子が今もお茶碗を両手で持っていること、力加減を覚えて、おもちゃや遊び道具を注意して扱うようになったことなどが認（したた）められていました。

Restoring a Rice Bowl
A boy's request

A few years ago, a couple and their two sons from Kobe visited my studio. The older son was a rambunctious second grader and the younger one was in kindergarten.

The boys had matching rice bowls with popular characters printed on them, and they loved them very much, but the older boy accidentally chipped his precious rice bowl in one day. He was very disappointed, and had come to the workshop because he wanted to restore it somehow.

I held the chipped rice bowl in my hands in front of him, and estimated the restoration price.

My estimates are simply based on the degree of damage, with set prices for one chip, one crack, etc., and no consideration of the value of the actual bowl. The chip in his bowl was not very large, but it was noticeable, and the estimate came to about 15,000 yen.

I explained to him the process of restoration and the time it would take to complete it, and proposed the decoration of "sprinkling gold" at the end as the bowl's reward for its patience in dealing with its having painfully been chipped.

At first, the boy thought that he could probably get the bowl restored easily and for just a few hundred yen, but as I explained the mounting costs in my estimate, his face became increasingly worried. When I told him that the total cost would be 15,000 yen, he looked dumbfounded.

But I didn't miss his mother smiling behind him with a "just as I thought" look on her face. The boy paid for the restoration out of his New Year's monetary gift, and two months later, when the restoration was completed, he came to pick up the bowl with his family.

The rice bowl, now beautifully restored by kintsugi, was even more captivating than before it was chipped.

"Thank you very much," the boy said to me.

"I fixed it beautifully," I said. "I'm sure the bowl will be very happy."

I noticed that the little boy was holding the bowl with both hands.

I then looked at the mother, who was smiling at her son, just as she had done when I gave him the estimate.

A short time later, I received a polite thank you letter from the parents. They wrote that their son has still been holding the bowl with both hands, and that he had learned to handle toys and playthings with care.

Column 3 コラム

清川先生と歩く | 漆芸舎スタッフ 渡邉 浩之

　清川先生は、昼食の後、たまに私を散歩に連れて行ってくれます。ここでは、先生から教えてもらった印象深い話をご紹介します。

とあるお寺の門

　あるお寺の門は、地の黒色に茶色の刷毛目がかなり目立って見えて、これは作為的なものか、それにしてはちょっと……と考えていると、清川先生が野外の塗装に用いる胡粉下地や、丹塗りの「塗りムラ」について教えてくれました。

　寺の門は木材の防腐のために、膠(動物の骨や皮を原料とした接着剤)と胡粉(牡蠣殻を粉末状にすりつぶしたもの)を混ぜた塗料で、もともと白く塗られています。この塗装を胡粉下地と言います。

　長い年月が経つと、胡粉下地は退色して剥がれ落ち、剥き出しになった木材には汚れが染み込んで、門全体が黒ずんでいきます。染み込んだ汚れは容易に落とせないことから、黒ずんだ門に胡粉下地をもう一度施し、再度防腐を行います。ところが、年月とともに、塗りが厚い部分は白色が残り、薄い部分は退色して黒色の汚れた地が現れてくるとのことでした。その結果、刷毛目が目立つくらいの塗りムラが出現してしまうのです。

　塗りムラは、彩色が行われた直後は誰にも分かりません。50年ほどで胡粉下地の退色が始まるため、職人の腕前は長い年月の後、明らかになるのです。「漆塗りにしても胡粉下地にしても、職人にとって塗りの仕事は怖いんだ。だって仕事の良し悪しが本人の隠居後に分かってしまうからね」と先生は言います。

Episode | By Hiroshi Watanabe, senior manager of Kiyokawa Lacquerware Art

Walking with Mr. Kiyokawa

After lunch, Mr. Kiyokawa sometimes has me accompany him on his walks.
Since Daitokuji Temple is right in front of our studio, we often walk around its precincts.

A certain temple gate

The gate leading to the precincts of the temple looked quite conspicuous, with brown brush marks on a black ground, and I was wondering if this was artificial or if it was a bit of a problem.

I'd been thinking about it for a while, when Mr. Kiyokawa taught me about the unevenness of the gofun undercoating.

The gates of temples are originally painted white with a mixture of nikawa animal glue and skins and gofun (oyster shells ground into a powder) to protect the wood. This coat of paint is called the "gofun undercoating." Over the years, the gofun undercoating fades and peels off, and grime sinks into the bare wood, darkening the entire gate. Since the stains cannot be easily removed, the darkened gate is re-coated with gofun undercoating, to once again protect the wood. However, as the years go by, the thickly coated areas remain white, while the lighter areas fade, exposing the black-stained ground. As a result, the unevenness of the paint application becomes noticeable.

The unevenness of the paint is not apparent to anyone immediately after the painting is done. After about fifty years, the undercoat begins to fade, so the skill of the craftsman becomes apparent. That's why Mr. Kiyokawa says, "Whether it is lacquer or gofun undercoating, the work of painting is scary. The quality of the craftsman's work will be known after he retires."

木がやせる

　工房の目の前が大徳寺なので、その境内をよく歩きます。ある日、一緒に歩いていると先生は門のところで立ち止まって門柱の木を触りました。私も同じように触れてみると、木目のざらついた感触が手に残ります。先生はこれを「木目が立っている」と言いますが、木目の感触でその木が何十年、何百年前のものか分かるそうです。「木目が立つ」ことを「木がやせる」とも言いますが、年月が経つと木目の間の柔らかい部分の水分が抜けて乾燥し、収縮していくことを示しています。ただし、「木がやせる＝木の強度が落ちる」ということではありません。

　古材は、時間をかけて自然に乾燥しながら同時に強度を増していきます。ある研究によると、樹齢100年で伐採されたヒノキは、次の100年後まで引っ張り強度（木材の端と端を左右に引っ張った時の耐久性）、圧縮強度が徐々に増していき、その後それらの強度がゆっくりと低下し、伐採から300年後にようやく伐採時と同じ強度になるようです。

　つまり、寺院の柱がやせていても、それは表面だけのことであって、中心部分は強度を高めており、1000年くらい過ぎていても全く問題ないそうです。実際、京都の東寺に四つある門（北・北大門、北東・慶賀門、南東・東大門〈不開門〉、西・蓮花門）はいずれも1000年以上前の建築ですが、今も立派に残っています。

　昔の職人は、屋根裏に建立当時の木材をストックしていました。200年、300年先の修復に必要だからです。寺院の修理は同じくらい年月が経っている木材で行わないと、強度はもちろん木材内部の密度や水分も異なるため、うまくいかないのです。

　そして、木の表面の「やせ」を隠すことができるのが漆塗りです。漆塗りによって木のやせを遅らせることはできますが、漆はさすがに1000年は持ちません。そのため、寺院では200〜300年に一回、古い漆の掻き落としを行い、柱を白木の状態に戻して下地からもう一度漆塗をやり直す大修復が行われるのです。

Wood becomes thin

Once when I was walking around Daitokuji Temple with Mr. Kiyokawa, he stopped at one gate and touched the wood of the gate pillar.

When he touches it, he says, he feels the rough texture of the wood grain on his hand. He says that he can tell if the wood is tens or hundreds of years old by the feel of the grain. The grain of the wood sometimes begins to stand out in a process called "trees becoming thin." As the years go by, the soft parts between the grains of the wood lose moisture, dry out, and shrink. However, the strength of the wood is not diminished.

Old wood dries naturally over time and gains strength at the same time. According to one study, cypress trees cut down at the age of one hundred years will gradually increase in tensile strength (the durability of the wood when pulled from side to side, end to end) and compressive strength for the next hundred years, after which the strength of the wood will slowly decrease until it finally reaches the same strength as when it was cut down, three hundred years later.

Therefore, even if the pillars of a temple have gotten lean, this is only a superficial quality. The central part of the pillar has increased its strength, and there is no problem at all, even if it is over a thousand years old. In fact, the four gates of Toji Temple in Kyoto — its Hokudai-mon in the north, Keiga-mon in the northeast, Todai-mon in the southeast, and Renka-mon in the west — were all built more than a thousand years ago, but they are perfectly intact today.

In the past, craftsmen stored stocks of wood from the time of construction in the attic. This was because they would need it for restoration two or three hundred years down the road. Temple repairs would not work unless they were done with wood that was the same age, because the density and moisture inside the wood would be different, as well as the strength.

Urushi lacquering can also hide the "wane" of the wood surface. Although lacquering can slow down the deterioration of the wood, the lacquer will not last for a thousand years. Therefore, every two to three hundred years, temples undergo a major restoration where the old lacquer is scraped off, the pillars are returned to their original state of white wood, and the lacquer is reapplied from the ground up.

京都の空き地や朽ちた神社で過ごす

　先生は時々、旧家を取り壊した後の空き地に足を向けます。空き地を見つけて、地面を指で少し穿ると、昔のタイルの破片や器のかけらが出てきます。かけらについた土を払って陽に当ててみると、きれいな模様が浮かび上がります。先生は模様を見ながら、昔この場所は風呂場だったとか、炊事場だったなどと話します。

　かけらを持ち帰り、周りを錆漆で固めて下地漆を塗った後、色漆や金で装飾するとちょっとしたアクセサリーになります。先生も私もひとしきり空き地を穿りながら、昔のかけらを探しますが、私たちが探しているかけらたちはきっと「時のおとしもの」なのです。それは完成しないジグソーパズルのピースのようですが、小さなピースから当時の人々の生活をイメージして思いを馳せ、パズルの完成図を想像します。かけらに行う金継ぎは、時のおとしものを封じ込めるタイムカプセルなのかもしれません。

　また、先生は工房近くの今は誰も顧みない朽ち果てた神社に私を連れて行ってくれたことがあります。弁柄漆の朱色が剥げて地肌が剥き出しになっている大鳥居を二人して眺め、塗装が剥げて放置されている本堂を歩きます。京都には、財政的な理由から人の手が入らず、廃墟になっている神社仏閣が少なからずある、と先生は言います。大事なことは、廃墟が撤去される前に、それらを造っている古材を保管しておくことだと教えてくれました。長い時を経た古材は二度と手に入らず、きちんと保管しておけば、現存している古い建物の補修に有効利用できるのです。

　私は、朽ちていく大鳥居を見上げて、ここにも「時のおとしもの」を見つけたように思いました。

Spending time in vacant lots and decaying shrines in Kyoto

Sometimes Mr. Kiyokawa goes to vacant lots after the old houses have been demolished. When he finds a vacant lot and digs a little into the ground with his fingers, he finds pieces of old tiles and vessels. When he removes the soil from the pieces and exposes them to the sun, beautiful designs emerge.

Looking at the designs, he tells us for instance that this place used to be a bathhouse, or it use to be a kitchen. We take the pieces home, harden them with sabi-urushi, paint them with base lacquer, and then decorate them with colored lacquer and gold to make little accessories. Mr. Kiyokawa and I spend some time digging around in the vacant lots, looking for little pieces of the past, certain we can find and salvage some little souvenirs of time. They are like the pieces of a jigsaw puzzle that will never be completed, but from the small pieces we can imagine the lives of the people of that time, and picture the completed puzzle. Maybe decorating remnants with kintsugi is like making a small time-capsule to contain the items of a lost era.

Mr. Kiyokawa once took me to a dilapidated shrine near his studio, a shrine that no one cares about anymore. We both gazed at the big torii gate, where the vermilion bengara lacquer had peeled away to expose the bare wood, and walked around the main hall, where the paint had all peeled away. The building was abandoned. There are not a few shrines and temples in Kyoto that have fallen into disrepair due to lack of human intervention for financial reasons, says Mr. Kiyokawa. And he advised me that the important thing is to salvage and stone thier old building materials before they are scrapped. The old timbers will never be available again, and if stored properly, they can be used to repair the old buildings that are still standing.

As I looked up at the decaying torii gate, I felt as if I had found here another possible "souvenir of time."

四章 | Chapter 4
私の金継ぎ修復の工程
My Kintsugi Restoration Process

私の金継ぎ修復の工程 | My Kintsugi Restoration Process

修復のデザイン
Design

器と向き合う

　金継ぎ修復に入る前に、まずは修復する器とじっくり向き合います。

　「壊れ」から「新たな景色」を創り上げるために、私は修復する器と持ち主の方との思い出や、その方の器への愛着をよく聞きこみます。もし器が自分のものであったなら、これまでどのように器と向き合ってきたか、作業前によく考え、さらに器のデザインや個性、作家や職人の想い、年代物の器であれば、どのような経緯をたどって、今、自分の元にやってきたのかを想像してみるのも楽しいです。

　例えば、古物商には、欠けてしまった江戸時代のそば猪口がよくありますが、器から昔の人の息吹が伝わるようで、それを買い求めて金継ぎしている間、私はちょっとした時間旅行を楽しんでいます。

　器と向き合う時間を経て金継ぎ修復のデザインがイメージできたら、割れ欠け部分に水性ペンを使って、想いのかたちを描いてみます。

First, contemplate the vessel

Before starting kintsugi restoration, we must carefully consider the vessel to be restored.

In order to create a "new landscape" from "brokenness," before starting the restoration work, I first listen carefully to the history of the vessel, and assess the owner's relationship to it. If the vessel is my own, I think about my own relationship with it. I also enjoy imagining the personality of the vessel, and what thoughts may have inspired the artist or craftsman at the time of its creation. If it is a vintage vessel, I also contemplate how it came to be with me.

I often find chipped soba-choku from the Edo period at antique shops. Gazing upon them, and holding them in my hands, I feel as if I can almost feel the breath of the people who used them so long ago.

Once I have spent some time with the vessel and have an idea of the design for the kintsugi restoration, I use a water-based pen to draw the shape I want on the cracks and chips.

If the vessel is broken into multiple pieces, I temporarily fix the broken parts with masking tape to recreate the original shape of the vessel. Then I place a piece of white paper next to the vessel and draw an image of what it will look

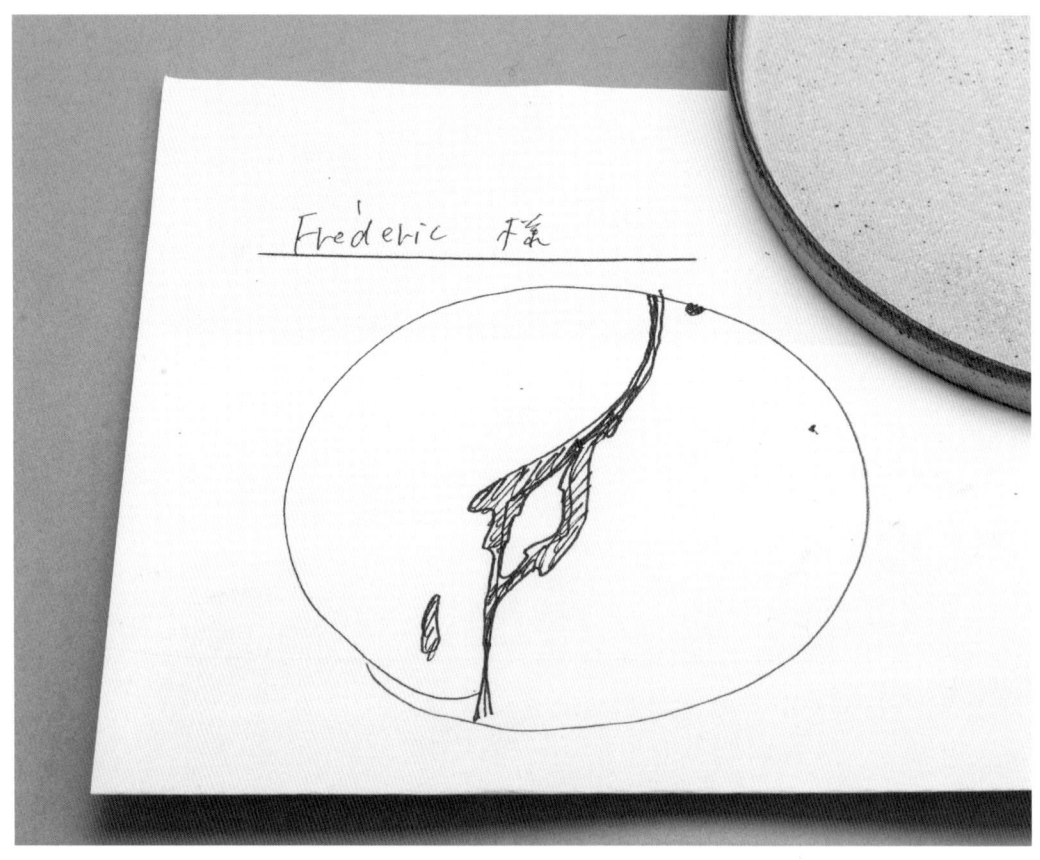

　器が複数に割れている場合は、割れ部分にマスキングテープを貼って仮留めし、器の本来のかたちを再現します。そして器の横に白い紙を置いて、修復後のイメージを描きます。いわば修復の「設計図づくり」です。

　小さな欠け（チップ）であれば、仕上がりが金の雫に見えるようにデザインしても良いですし、急須や片口の口が欠けていたら、欠け部分から金がこぼれ出ているような「垂れ」のデザインをしても良いでしょう。

欠けのかたちが面白かったら、それを動物や植物に見立ててデザインしますし、必ずしも金で継ごうとは思わず、色漆などで仕上げる場合もあります。

　割れ、ひびの場合は、シンプルに継ぐ修復が一般的ですが、例えば割れた器に唐草模様が描かれていたら、修復で継ぎ合わせる部分の線の最後を唐草のように丸めてみて、器の模様と金継ぎの調和を創るデザインを考えたりします。

　大きな割れや欠けの場合、器が男性的

like after restoration. This is a kind of "blueprint" of the restoration.

If the chip is small, it can be designed to look like a drop of gold. If a chip occurs in the mouth of a teapot or a katakuchi (spouted bowl), I might design it to look as if gold were spilling out from the chip. If the shape of the chip is interesting, I can design it to look like an animal or a plant. If needed I can also use various colored lacquers in place of gold.

In the case of cracks and fissures, the most common method is to simply repair the joint, but if the broken vessel has an arabesque pattern, for example, I might try to round off the tail of the joint to create a design that harmonizes with the original pattern of the vessel.

In the case of a large crack or chip, if the vessel has a masculine design, I might heap up sabi-urushi on the joint to form a little mountain range. On such a surface the gold will shine three-dimensionally when the vessel is illuminated. Accentuating the natural contour of the breakage, I may shape the gold to look like a bolt of lightning.

私の金継ぎ修復の工程　｜　My Kintsugi Restoration Process

修復のデザイン
Design

なデザインのものであれば、私は継ぎ部分に錆漆を盛り上げて山脈のように形作り、金蒔き終了後、器に光が当たった時に金が立体的に輝くようにします。割れによっては、継ぎ目を稲妻(いなずま)のように見せることもあります。

私が心がけていること

　金継ぎのデザインを考えるうえで、心がけていることがあります。それは、「金継ぎ修復が器より前に出てはいけない（目立ってはいけない）」ということです。金継ぎ修復は、器に寄り添い、器の持つ個性を引き立てるためにあるからです。

　金継ぎの技法のひとつに「呼び継ぎ」という、ある器の欠けた部分に別の壊れた器の欠けを組み合わせて修復する技法があります。呼び継ぎも古くから伝わっている技法で、名品も数多く残されていますし、優れた技術であることは間違いないのですが、私自身は進んで行おうとは思っていません。

なぜなら、欠けを補(おぎな)うために組み合わさされた器のそれぞれの作り手は、自分の器が他の器と合わさることを望むのか、という疑問に捉(とら)われるからです。呼び継ぎは修復ではなく、直す人の創作性が表れる「作品」であり、この点で、呼び継ぎは器より修復の個性が前に出てしまう技法なのです。

　いずれにしても、金継ぎは単なる器の欠け、割れの修復ではありません。繰り返しますが、持ち主の想い、作り手の想い、器の個性、歴史の全てを詰め込んで、壊れてしまった器に「新しい景色」と「いのち」を与えることが金継ぎ修復です。そして私が、漆、米粉、砥の粉、金粉などの自然素材を使用することにこだわるのは、自然素材こそが器を最も長く後世に残す材料であり、やがて遠い将来、再び器の寿命が訪れた時、全てが土にかえることができる材料であるからです。

What I keep in mind

One thing I try to keep in mind when I design kintsugi is that the restoration should not be more noticeable than the vessel to be restored. Such an imbalance would betray the very purpose of kintsugi restoration: to conserve the nature of the vessel and enhance its individuality.

One of the specialties used in kintsugi is "yobitsugi," a technique of repairing a broken piece of vessel by combining it with another broken piece. This technique is centuries old, and many masterpieces represent its legacy, so there is no doubt that it is an excellent technique. I myself, however, am not willing to use it, because I cannot help wondering if the makers of the individual vessels would actually want their work to be treated this way. I tend to consider yobitsugi a technique in which the individuality of the restorer precedes the individuality of the vessel.

In any case, kintsugi is more than just repairing chipped or cracked vessels. Again, the very purpose of kintsugi is to give a new "landscape" and "life" to a so-called "broken" vessel by creatively incorporating many strands of its identity: the owner's memories, the maker's inspiration, the vessel's personality, and the happenstances of history.

I always use natural materials such as lacquer, rice powder, abrasive powder, and gold powder. The reason why I insist on using natural materials is because they can preserve the vessel and its intricate relationships for the longest time, and can be returned to the earth when the life of the vessel finally reaches its natural end.

私の金継ぎ修復の工程 ｜ My Kintsugi Restoration Process

金継ぎに使用する道具
Tools

基本の道具 ｜ Basic tools

金継ぎ修復は、七つの基本道具で行うことができます。
Kintsugi restoration can be done with seven basic tools.

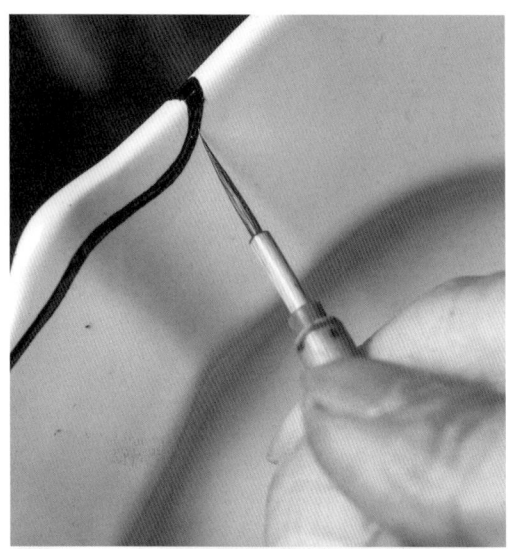

1 ｜ 面相筆 ｜ Menso Fude
Fine point brush

小さな割れ欠けの継ぎ目やひびの修復の際に行う黒漆を使った中塗り、上塗り、金蒔き前の弁柄漆塗りに使用します。「面相」の名前の通り、眉、目尻、口元など表情を描く細筆で、毛先は天然のイタチ毛で作られています。

This brush is used to apply kuro-urushi to delicate areas such as the joints of small chips and fissures. As the name suggests, it is a fine brush used by doll makers to draw facial details such as the eyebrows, and the corners of the eyes and mouth. The hairs of the brush are of weasel hair.

2 ｜ 毛棒 ｜ Kebo
Brush for sowing gold powder

金蒔きの際、毛棒で金粉をすくって弁柄漆の上に蒔きます。毛先はタヌキ毛が用いられています。

This small brush is used to scoop up the gold powder and sprinkled it onto the lacquer. The hairs of the brush are of tanuki (raccoon dog) hair.

3 | 平筆 | Hira Fude
Flat brush

面相筆が細かい部分を塗ることに適しているのに対し、平筆は割れ欠け部分の面積が大きい場所を塗る時に使用します。京都産の竹を割り、その間に和紙と共に馬の毛を挟み、絹糸で縛ったものです。

While the fine point brush is used to paint small areas, the flat brush is used to paint large areas of chips and cracks. The bristles are made of horsehair, placed between split slats of bamboo and Japanese paper. The paper functions as a kind of cushion and support for the horsehair, and the whole is bound firmly with silk thread.

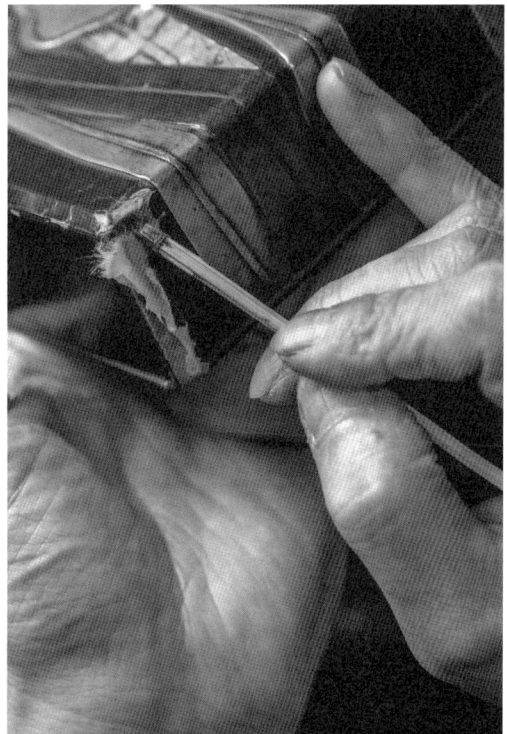

4 | 檜箆 | Hinoki Hera
Japanese cypress spatula

のり漆と錆漆をつくる時、漆と米粉、漆と砥の粉を混ぜるのに使います。檜は軟らかく、しなりがよいため、漆と米粉、漆と砥の粉を定盤の上で混ぜるのに向いています。

A hinoki (Japanese cypress) spatula is used to mix the lacquer and rice powder, or lacquer and powdered clay, when making nori-urushi and sabi-urushi, respectively. Since hinoki is soft and pliable, it is suitable for mixing these constituents on the wooden slate that serves as a palette.

5 | 竹箆 | Take Hera
Bamboo spatula

のり漆や錆漆を器の欠けた断面部分に付ける時に使います。先端を丸くして、割れ欠けの断面に沿わせやすいようにしています。

A bamboo spatula is used to apply nori-urushi or sabi-urushi to the repaired part of the vessel. The tip of the spatula is rounded so that the urushi can easily be applied to the cross sections of cracks and chips.

6 | 定盤 | Joban
Wooden slate

定盤の上でのり漆や錆漆をつくります。素材は朴木で、版画などによく使われますが、木目がきれいで丈夫であるのが特長です。使い込まれた定盤は漆がたくさん沁み込んでおり、表面が鏡面のように光ります。

Nori-urushi and sabi-urushi are made on a wooden slate. The material of the slate is magnolia wood, which is very strong due to its beautiful, even grain. Magnolia is often used for woodblock prints. When a wooden slate has been used for a long time, it absorbs a great quantity of lacquer, and its surface becomes shiny like a mirror.

7 ｜ 白磁の小皿
White porcelain dish

のり漆、錆漆、黒漆、弁柄漆などは白磁の小皿に載せて使います。白い小皿の上で行うこのは、漆の具合（色、濃度）を観察しやすいからです。

To use the blended urushi, it is transferred onto a small white porcelain dish. A white dish is used, because it makes it easier to observe the condition (color and density) of the lacquer.

京の手習い 金継ぎ教室について ｜ About My Kintsugi Workshops

私は京都と東京で金継ぎ教室を主宰しています。金継ぎを通して江戸時代から続く職人技術を少しでも多くの方に伝授することで、伝統技法の承継を行いたいと思っています。教室では、漆をはじめ、全て日本産の自然素材を使用し、私が厳選した日本製の道具で勉強していただきます。私が漆も道具も日本産にこだわるのは、それを使ってもらうことで日本の職人文化を維持したいからです。教室に通うコースの他、2時間ほどで金継ぎの概要を知ることができる体験コースを設けています。

I run kintsugi classes in Kyoto and Tokyo. Through kintsugi, I would like to pass on the traditional techniques to the future by teaching as many people as possible the craftsmanship that has continued since the Edo period. In my classes, I use only natural materials from Japan, including lacquer, and carefully selected tools made in Japan. The reason why I insist on using only Japanese lacquer and tools is because I want to maintain the culture of Japanese craftsmanship by having people use them. I also offer a hands-on course where you can get an overview of kintsugi in about two hours.

私の金継ぎ修復の工程 | My Kintsugi Restoration Process

漆との付き合い方
How to get along with lacquer

金継ぎに不可欠な三つの漆
The three urushi lacquers essential for kintsugi

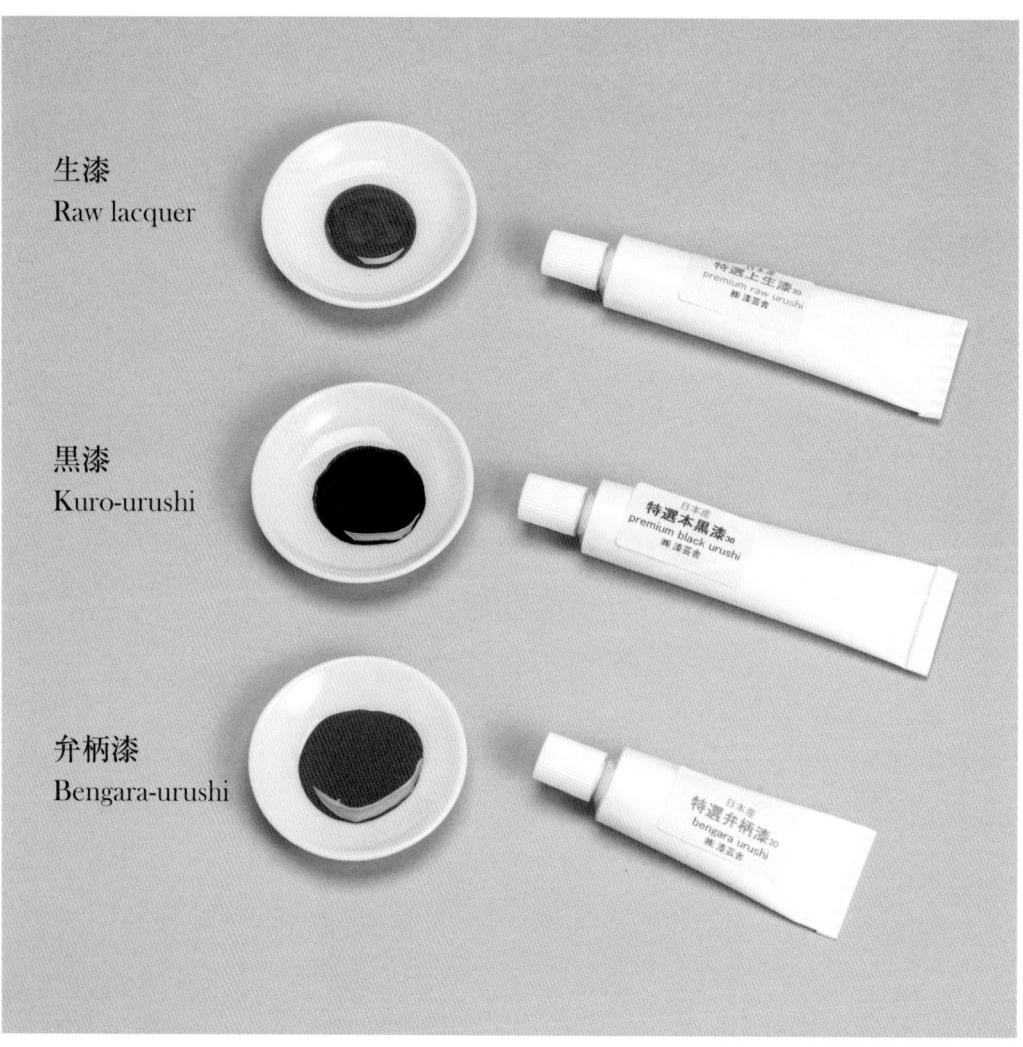

生漆
Raw lacquer

黒漆
Kuro-urushi

弁柄漆
Bengara-urushi

生漆 (きうるし)

生漆は、漆の木から採取した樹液に混じっているごみを濾過(ろか)して除去したものです。水分が多く乾燥するのが早いため、のり漆、錆漆、下地、拭(ふ)き漆などに使われますが、塗りには使われません。

黒漆 (くろうるし)

黒漆は生漆にとても細かい鉄粉(または水酸化鉄)を混ぜて、漆の成分と鉄粉の酸化作用により漆を黒くしたものです。昔は鉄漿(てっしょう)(お歯黒)を混ぜていました。

金継ぎ修復では、主に下地塗り(中塗り、上塗り)に使用します。よく使う「漆黒(しっこく)」という言葉は、黒漆を塗った漆器のような深い艶(つや)のある黒色のことです。

弁柄漆 (べんがらうるし)

金蒔きする部分の下絵として塗るのが弁柄漆です。弁柄とは土からとれる酸化鉄を主成分とする赤色顔料(がんりょう)のことで、その語源はインドのベンガル地方から伝来したことに由ります。日本の暮らしに古くから根づいている伝統的な色漆で、陶器や漆器に使われることはもちろん、経年劣化に強く日光による褪色(たいしょく)がないことや防虫、防腐の効果が高いことから、家屋(かおく)の塗装にも使われてきました。

Raw lacquer

Raw lacquer, referred to as "ki-urushi," is made by filtering out the debris mixed in the sap collected from the urushi tree. It has a high water content and short drying time, and is used as a base for nori-urushi, sabi-urushi, undercoating, simple fuki-urushi "wiped-on lacquer," etc.

Kuro-urushi

Kuro-urushi is made by mixing very fine iron powder (or iron hydroxide) with raw lacquer, which blackens the lacquer through the oxidizing effect of the iron powder. In kintsugi restoration, kuro-urushi is mainly used as a base coat (middle coat and top coat). The term "urushi black" refers to a deep, glossy black color, like lacquerware coated with kuro-urushi, "black lacquer."

Bengara-urushi

Bengara-urushi is used as the ground onto which the gold issown. The word "bengara" refers to a red pigment composed mainly of iron oxide, and its name comes from the old Japanese word for the Bengal region of India, from where the pigment was first introduced to Japan. Bengara has been used in Japan for a long time, not only by the craftwork specialists of pottery and lacquer ware, but also by common folk. It was used for painting houses, because it is highly durable, does not fade, and is highly effective as an insecticide and antiseptic.

私の金継ぎ修復の工程 ｜ My Kintsugi Restoration Process
漆との付き合い方
How to get along with lacquer

漆かぶれについて

　漆は劇薬ではないので、触ってもすぐにかぶれることはありません。その人の体質によりますが、少なくとも、かぶれるまで1〜2時間ほどかかります。もともと漆は樹液であり、人間で言う血液のようなものです。漆の木を守るため、血液が身体を守るように「かさぶた」を形成しようとします。漆が人間の皮膚に付着した場合でも、固まろうと作用し身体が反応することでかぶれが起こるのです。かぶれはすぐに生じないので油断して、漆粉（余分なのり漆を取り除く時と錆漆を研ぐ時に発生するもの）の片づけや手洗いをせず、漆粉がついたままの手で無意識に目や口を触ったりするのは良くありません。

　かぶれを防ぐ方法は、作業開始前に白い紙を作業机の上に敷いて、漆粉が机上に落ちた際にそれを「見える化」し、掃除をしやすくすることです。

　また、作業は必ず使い捨てのビニール手袋やアームカバーを腕に着けて行うことで、生漆が指先についたり、漆粉が直接皮膚に触れないようにすることに加え、漆粉が着衣に付着することも予防できます。

　のり漆の掃除や錆漆の研ぎは、常に水を少量入れた小皿を横に置き、鑢を濡らしてから行います。このように「水研ぎ」をすることで、漆粉の飛散を防げます。

　もし漆が手や腕についた場合は、少量のテレピン油で漆を落とした後、石鹸で手を洗い、ハンドクリームを塗っておけばかぶれることはありません。

On lacquer poisoning

Lacquer is not actually a poisonous substance, and contact with it will not result in an immediate rash. It depends on the person's constitution, but in cases of an allergic reaction it will take at least one to two hours for a rash to develop. Basically, lacquer begins as sap, and that sap will form a hard covering over the tree's injuries just as blood forms a scab to protect the human body. Somehow lacquer also hardens when it touches people's skin, and this causes a rash in some people.

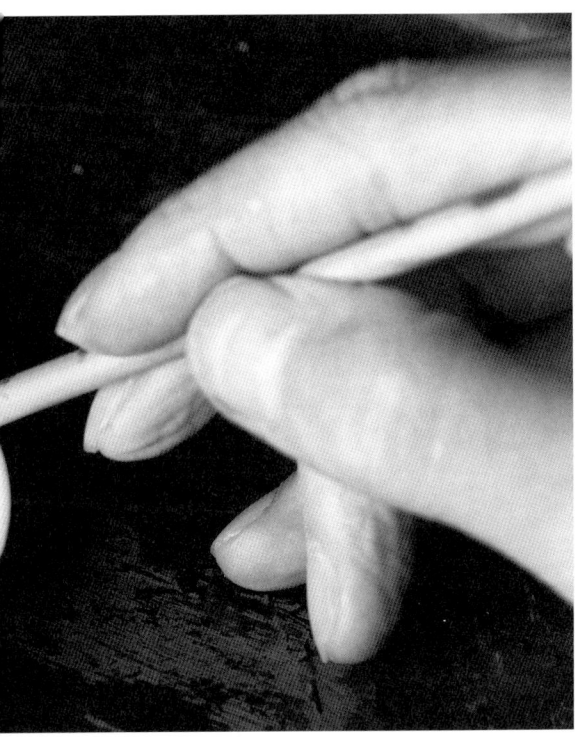

It is advisable to avoid touching your eyes or mouth if there is a likelihood that lacquer powder resides on your hands, for the very reason that an allergic reaction will not occur immediately. Once you notice it may be too late.

Lacquer powder is generated upon removal of excess nori-urushi, for example, or when sabi-urushi is sanded down. A good way to prevent a rash is to place a piece of white paper on your desk before you start working so that you can see where the lacquer powder falls, making it easier to clean.

Always wear disposable vinyl gloves and arm covers to prevent raw lacquer from touching your fingertips and lacquer powder from coming into direct contact with your skin. It also prevents lacquer powder from getting on your clothes.

When cleaning nori-urushi or sanding down sabi-urushi, always keep a small water dish at hand and wet the file before working. This prevents the lacquer powder from scattering.

If the lacquer gets on your hands or arms, remove it with a small amount of turpentine oil, wash your hands and arms thoroughly with soap, and apply hand cream to avoid a rash.

私の金継ぎ修復の工程 | My Kintsugi Restoration Process

漆との付き合い方
How to get along with lacquer

漆の酸化を防ぐ
Preventing the oxidation of lacquer

漆は空気に触れた瞬間から酸化して硬化が始まります。したがって、漆を小皿の上で放置しておくと、すぐに使えなくなります。貴重な漆を無駄にしないために、次のことを心がけます。

Lacquer oxidizes and begins to harden the moment it comes into contact with air. If you leave lacquer on a plate, it will soon become unusable. In order to avoid wasting precious lacquer, keep the following in mind:

1 | 漆は必要な量を、できる限り作業の直前に小皿または定盤に出し、使い切ります。

Immediately before working, dispense only the necessary amount of lacquer onto the small dish or onto the joban (the wooden slate used for making nori-and sabi-urushi), and try to use it all in one session.

2 | のり漆（右頁参照）、錆漆（121頁参照）は定盤の上で手早くつくり、できあがったら小皿に移してラップで覆い、ラップ内の空気を外に出して密閉します。黒漆、色漆についても、小皿に出したら同様にラップをかけます。
密閉することで酸化を抑えることができ、ラップ内の空気を抜いておくことにより、翌日くらいまで使うことが可能です。

Work swiftly when making the nori-urushi (see page 119) or sabi-urushi (see page 121) on the joban, and when it is done, transfer it onto the small dish and cover it with plastic wrap to keep the air out. For kuro-urushi and iro-urushi (colored lacquer), wrap them in the same way after placing them onto the small dish. The plastic wrap will protect the lacquer from the air, and the lacquer can be used until the next day or so.

「のり漆」について

　かけらをくっつけるために必要な接着剤が「のり漆」です。私のつくるのり漆には必ず米粉を使います。生漆1に対して米粉1の割合で調合します。なぜ米粉を使うのかというと、日本の稲作文化は豊かで、食生活の中心に米があるからです。昔の人は器の割れ欠けを直すのに、米を炊いた鍋にこびりついて残ったごはん粒と漆を混ぜて接着剤にして使っていました。米粉と生漆の調合が最適であるという答えは、日本の生活文化から導かれていると思います。

About nori-urushi

I always use rice powder in my nori-urushi, with a 1:1 ratio of rice powder to raw lacquer. I use rice powder because Japan is a rice-growing country and rice is at the center of our diet. In the past, people used to mix lacquer with rice remnants from thier everyday-use container for cooked rice, to make an adhesive to repair cracks and chips in vessels. So, this mixture of rice powder and raw lacquer emerged from the culture of the Japanese lifestyle.

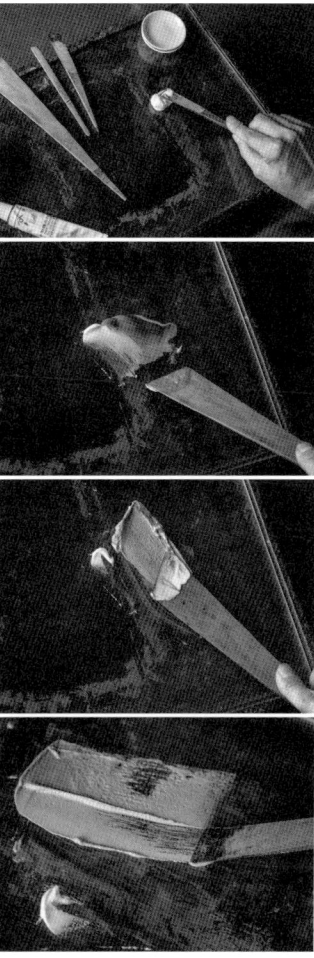

酸化する前の「のり漆」は生漆本来のベージュ色をしています。

Before oxidization, nori-urushi has the original color of raw lacquer, which is beige.

酸化が進んだ「のり漆」は色が黒ずみ、ダークブラウン色になります。

The color of nori-urushi that has been oxidized becomes darker, dark brown color.

私の金継ぎ修復の工程 | My Kintsugi Restoration Process

漆との付き合い方
How to get along with lacquer

捨て漆
Sute-urushi

のり漆を塗布する前に、接着する断面や鑢で荒らした表面に生漆を塗って、すぐに拭き取る作業「捨て漆」を行います。生漆を器に染み込ませることで、のり漆と器の接着の相性を良くし、接着強度と持続性を向上させることができます。

Applying raw lacquer to the cross sections of the places to be bonded, or to a surface that has been roughened with a file, and then wiping it off immediately is a technique called sute-urushi, "discarded lacquer." By letting the raw lacquer seep into the vessel, it improves the compatibility between nori-urushi and the vessel, and increases the strength and durability of the bond.

「喰い裂き」をのり漆に応用する
Applying "kuisaki" to nori-urushi

表具師は和紙と和紙を継ぐのに「喰い裂き」と呼ばれる技法を使います。和紙の端を水で濡らして繊維をほぐし引っ張るようにして引き裂く技法で、長い繊維を保つことができ、ほぐした繊維同士を絡ませて継ぐことで強度を高めます。器の修復においても接着強度を高める必要がある場合に和紙の繊維をのり漆に混ぜることがあります。

Hyogushi, traditional Japanese scroll mounters, use a technique called "kuisaki" to join sheets of washi (Japanese paper) together. Taking advantage of the fact that the fibers of washi are very long, hyogushi wet the edges of the sheets to be joined, loosen the fibers, and intertwine the fibers to join the sheets. In the restoration of vessels, when it is necessary to increase the strength of the bond, washi fibers are sometimes mixed with glue and lacquer.

「錆漆」について

　「錆漆」はのり漆の上に盛って、継ぎ目のかたちを形成するパテになります。錆漆は京都市山科で採れる砥の粉（山の土）と生漆を1対1の割合で混ぜてつくります。

　なぜのり漆の上に直接黒漆で下地塗りをせず錆漆を盛るのかというと、のり漆の米粉は時が経つと縮むのに対し、錆漆は収縮しない「土」を用いているため、かたちが変わることはないからです。

About sabi-rushi

Sabi-urushi is used as a putty on top of the nori-urushi to give form to the seam. While nori-urushi is made by mixing rice powder and raw lacquer, sabi-urushi is made by mixing raw lacquer and tonoko, powdered mountain clay from the Yamashina district in Kyoto prefecture, at a ratio of 1:1.

The reason why sabi-urushi is mounded on top of the nori-urushi instead of applying the kuro-urushi undercoating directly onto it is that the rice powder in nori-urushi shrinks over time, whereas sabi-urushi is a mixture of lacquer and dry clay, and so it does not shrink nor change its shape.

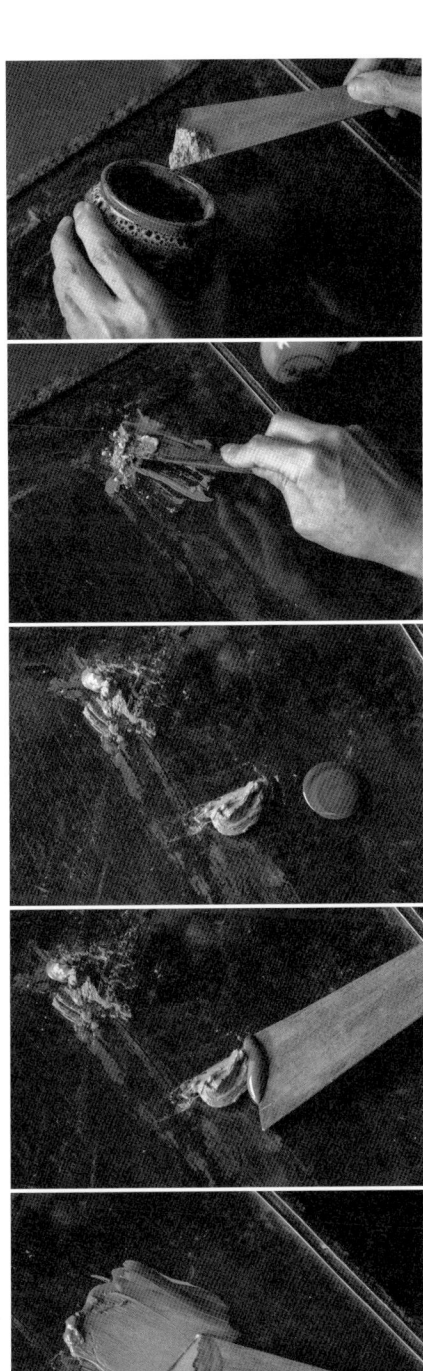

私の金継ぎ修復の工程 | My Kintsugi Restoration Process

「かすがい」による接着強化
Strengthening of adhesion with kasugai

　「かすがい」とは、もともと材木と材木とを繋ぎ留めるために打ち込む、両端の曲がった大釘のことで、ホッチキスの針のようなイメージです。金継ぎ修復では、二つに大きく割れた器や急須、マグカップの持ち手など重みのかかる箇所の割れに対し、のり漆による接着だけでは心もとないため、割れを跨ぐように竹や金属の「かすがい」を渡して補強します。この技法は古くから存在しており、第1章でご紹介した南宋時代の青磁茶碗「銘馬蝗絆」（29頁）は鉄のかすがいが施された名品です。

📖 page 29 — Chapter 1

青磁茶碗　銘　馬蝗絆
Celadon Tea Bowl "Bakohan" (Locust Bond)

page 38 — Chapter 2

生活文化と職人
The Roots of kintsugi in Everyday Life

Kasugai originated from the large nails with bent ends that were used to keep pieces of lumber together. Their shape resembles that of a staple. In kintsugi restoration, when a vessel is split in two, or when a handle of a teapot or cup is cracked in a place subject to a lot of weight, gluing with nori-urushi (glue lacquer) is not enough, so a bamboo or metal kasugai is passed across the crack to reinforce it. This technique has existed for a long time, and the celadon tea bowl "Bakohan (see page 29)," introduced in Chapter 1 is a representative masterpiece.

私の金継ぎ修復の工程 | My Kintsugi Restoration Process

金継ぎ修復の工程
The Steps in the Kintsugi Restoration Process

金継ぎ修復の基本工程 | Basic process

基本となる修復工程は次の6工程です。
The six basic steps are as follows:

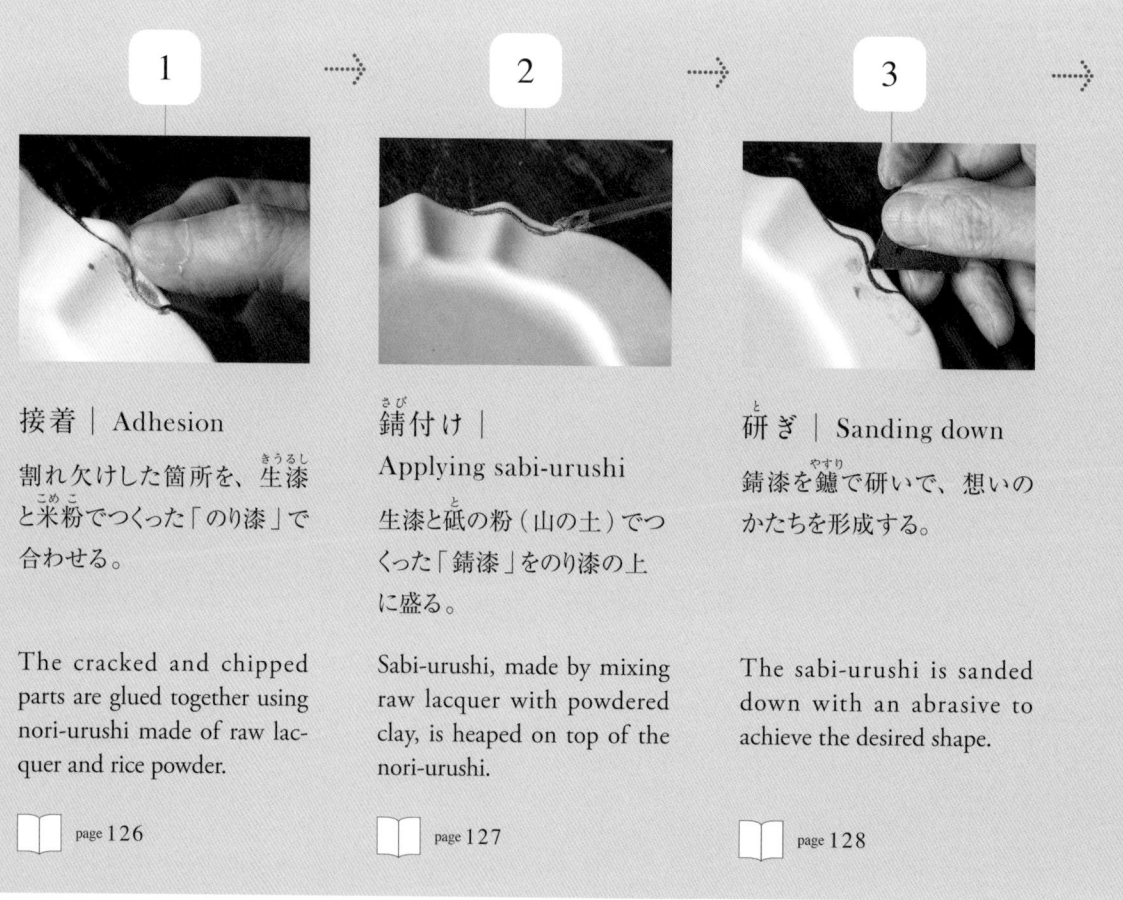

1 接着 | Adhesion

割れ欠けした箇所を、生漆（きうるし）と米粉（こめこ）でつくった「のり漆」で合わせる。

The cracked and chipped parts are glued together using nori-urushi made of raw lacquer and rice powder.

📖 page 126

2 錆付け | Applying sabi-urushi

生漆と砥の粉（と）（山の土）でつくった「錆漆」をのり漆の上に盛る。

Sabi-urushi, made by mixing raw lacquer with powdered clay, is heaped on top of the nori-urushi.

📖 page 127

3 研ぎ（と）| Sanding down

錆漆を鑢（やすり）で研いで、想いのかたちを形成する。

The sabi-urushi is sanded down with an abrasive to achieve the desired shape.

📖 page 128

各工程の間で、器を室（むろ）に置いて漆の乾燥を待ちます。乾燥の速度は各季節の温度、湿度によりますが、乾燥日数含めて完成まで2〜3か月ほどかかります。

私が行う金継ぎ修復の工程は江戸時代から続く職人技術を承継したもので、一部は私が応用して考えましたが、ほとんどは先人から教わったものです。
　ここでは、伝統工芸や修復工程を通して、金継ぎのさらなる魅力をご紹介します。

My process of kintsugi restoration is a living inheritance of the craftsmanship practiced in Japan since the Edo period (1603–1868). Some parts of this process are methods I have adapted or devised, but most of it I learned from my predecessors. In this chapter, I will introduce in more detail the fascinating techniques of kintsugi used in traditional crafts and restoration processes.

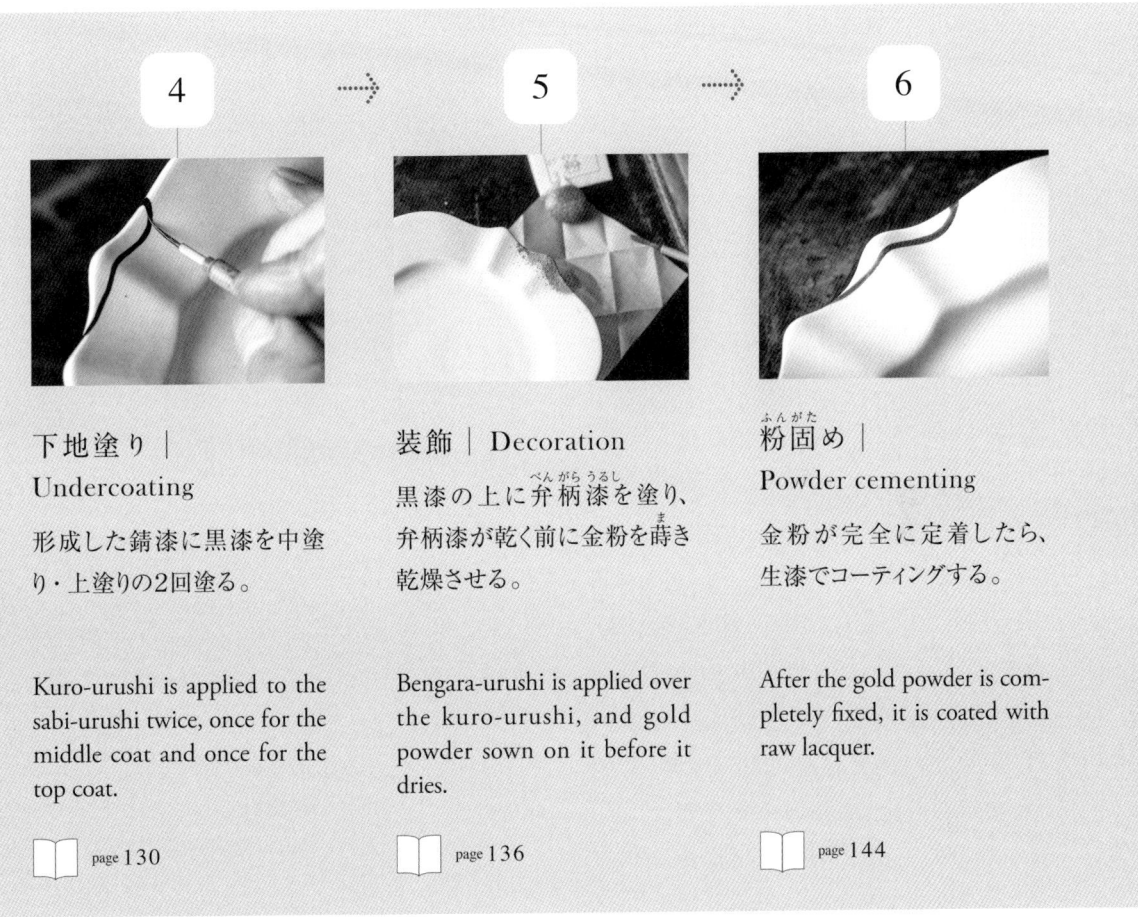

4 下地塗り | Undercoating
形成した錆漆に黒漆を中塗り・上塗りの2回塗る。

Kuro-urushi is applied to the sabi-urushi twice, once for the middle coat and once for the top coat.

page 130

5 装飾 | Decoration
黒漆の上に弁柄漆を塗り、弁柄漆が乾く前に金粉を蒔き乾燥させる。

Bengara-urushi is applied over the kuro-urushi, and gold powder sown on it before it dries.

page 136

6 粉固め | Powder cementing
金粉が完全に定着したら、生漆でコーティングする。

After the gold powder is completely fixed, it is coated with raw lacquer.

page 144

After each step in the process, the vessel is placed in the muro (chamber for drying the lacquer). The speed of drying depends on the temperature and humidity of the season, but it generally takes two to three months to complete the entire process.

私の金継ぎ修復の工程 | My Kintsugi Restoration Process

1 接着 | Adhesion

接着について

まず、捨て漆の作業を済ませてから、少しはみ出る程度ののり漆で割れ欠け部分を接着した後、マスキングテープで動かないように養生をします。のり漆の硬さは米粉に混ぜる水分で調整し、目の粗い陶器には「硬め」、目の詰まった磁器には「軟らかめ」ののり漆で接着します。接着直後にテレピン油を使って余分なのり漆を拭き取っておくと、後の作業が楽になります。3〜5日間、室で乾燥させた後、のり漆が硬化したことを確認して錆付けの作業に入ります。

The adhesion step

After the process of sute-urushi (discarded lacquer), nori-urushi is applied to the surface to be rejoined, using just enough of it that it comes out from the edges when you stick the parts together. Wipe off the excess nori-urushi with turpentine. Masking tape is used to prevent the parts from moving. The density of the nori-urushi is adjusted by the amount of water mixed with the rice powder. Thicker nori-urushi is used for coarse ceramics, and thinner nori-urushi is used for porcelain. After three to five days of drying in the muro, the adhesion is checked to confirm that it is hard, and the sabi-urushi application process begins.

私の金継ぎ修復の工程 | My Kintsugi Restoration Process

2 錆(さび)付け | Applying sabi-urushi

錆漆を盛る

錆漆を盛る時は、次の工程で行う「研ぎ」の作業を意識します。効率よくきれいに研ぎ上げるために、錆漆を盛る作業中に自分が思い描いた「新しい景色（＝デザイン）」を頭に浮かべながら、竹箆(たけべら)でかたちを整えつつ盛っていきます。錆漆を盛った器は室に入れて硬化させます。梅雨時期など湿度が高い時は、錆漆は1日ほどで硬化しますが、冬などの湿度が低い時期は日数がかかります。

Gauging the sabi-urushi

When applying the sabi-urushi, be aware of the sanding down process to be done later. To enable myself to accomplish the sanding down process neatly and efficiently, I shape the sabi-urushi with the bamboo spatula keeping in mind the "new scenery" (design) that I envision. After the sabi-urushi is applied, the vessel is placed in the muro. When the humidity is high, such as during the rainy season, the sabi-urushi takes about a day to harden. However, in winter, when the humidity is low, it takes longer.

私の金継ぎ修復の工程 | My Kintsugi Restoration Process

3 研(と)ぎ | Sanding down

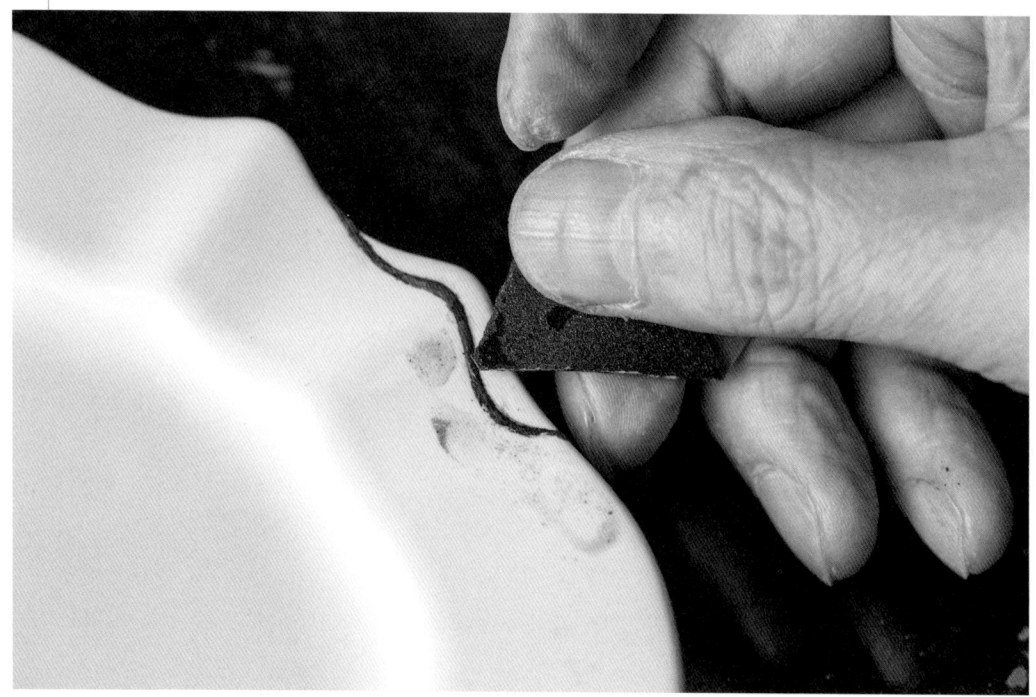

形成・研ぎ

　形成とは、乾いて硬化した錆漆を削り、次の工程で行う「下地塗り」の土台をつくることです。この作業を「錆研ぎ」と言い、表面を滑(なめ)らかにしつつ、かたちを整えることから「研ぐ」という言葉を使います。

　錆研ぎは地味で根気のいる作業ですが、私は金継ぎ修復の中で一番大事な工程だと思っています。それは錆研ぎをしっかり行ったか否(いな)かで、金蒔き後の仕上がりに差が出

Forming and sanding down

This is the process of shaving the dried and hardened sabi-urushi to form it into the desired shape and make the surface smooth, and to thus create the base for the coating with kuro-urushi. We refer to this process as "sabi togi."

Sabi togi is a simple but painstaking process, and I think this work is the most important in the entire kintsugi process. The quality of the finish after the gold is sown depends entirely on whether sabi togi is done properly or not. If not done properly, craters and small holes will remain, and even if gold is sown, it will not

るからです。錆研ぎが甘いとクレーターや小さな穴が残ってしまい、金を蒔いても美しく仕上がりません。最初に思い描いた新しい景色（デザイン）をうまくかたちにできるかどうかは、錆研ぎにかかっているとも言えます。

　錆研ぎは耐水ペーパーとアートナイフを用います。昔は器を傷つけにくい研ぎ用の駿河炭という炭を使っていましたが、今は良質なものが手に入りにくいことや炭自体のコンディションを整えないと上手く仕上がらないことから、現在は耐水ペーパーを使っています。

　研ぐ前に表面の凹凸の様子を水を垂らして確認し、耐水ペーパーを三角に折って、三角の先端で錆漆を研ぎます。アートナイフは主に錆漆のエッジの処理に使います。エッジがきれいに仕上がっていると金蒔きが美しくなります。

　「漆かぶれ」（116頁）でも述べましたが、錆研ぎの作業では漆粉が飛散するので、作業机に白い紙を敷いて粉の飛び散りが見えるようにします。作業中は使い捨てのビニール手袋とアームカバーを装着し、水研ぎで行います。

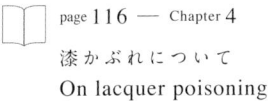

page 116 — Chapter 4
漆かぶれについて
On lacquer poisoning

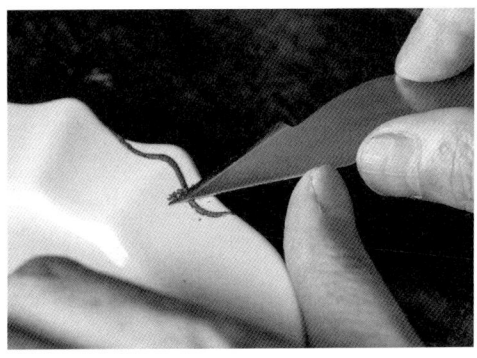

have a beautiful finish. Sabi togi determines whether or not the new scenery (design) envisioned at the beginning can be accomplished.

The sabi togi work is done with waterproof sandpaper and an art knife. In the past, we used a kind of charcoal called 'suruga sumi'. Charcoal is quite effective and does not damage the vessel, but nowadays, both because it is difficult to find good quality charcoal and because charcoal requires conditioning, I instead use waterproof sandpaper.

I check the unevenness of the surface by dripping water onto the sabi-urushi, then fold the sandpaper into a triangle and sand the wet surface down with the tip of the triangle. The art knife is manly used to treat the edges of the sabi-urushi. If the edges are neat, the finished kintsugi will be beautiful.

As I wrote in the section about "How to get along with lacquer (see page 116)," urushi powder tends to scatter about when sanding down the sabi-urushi, so I put white paper on my work table, enabling me to see the powder. During work, disposable vinyl gloves and arm covers are worn.

私の金継ぎ修復の工程 | My Kintsugi Restoration Process

4 下地塗り | Undercoating

下地塗り

形成(研ぎ)が終了したら、下地塗りに入ります。下地塗りは黒漆を使い、中塗りと上塗りの2回に分けて行います。面積が狭く、細い箇所を塗る時は面相筆、面積が広い箇所を塗る時には平筆を使用します。一般的には、漆を「塗る」と言いますが、私は、漆は「塗る」ものではなく「置く」もの、「配る」ものだと考えています。

黒漆を濾す

下地塗りを行う前に、基本的には黒漆を濾す作業をしますが、チューブからおろしたての新品な黒漆であれば濾す必要はありません。しかし、ひとたびチューブを開ければ、肉眼では見えにくい微量の塵が混じってしまいます。塵が混じったままの漆で器を塗ると、表面に気泡のようなプツプツができてしまい、きれいな仕上がりになりません。

そこで塵を取り除くために、濾紙を使って漉す作業をします。濾紙に黒漆を乗せ、そのまま紙の両端を指でつまんで、捻じっていきます。強く捻じると濾紙からきれいな漆が絞り出されます。

Applying the undercoating

When the sabi togi work is finished, the undercoating is applied. Kuro-urushi is used for it, and it involves applying the middle coat and the top coat. The menso fude is used for narrow areas, and the hira fude is used for large areas. I think of the matter of 'applying' the lacquer as a matter of placing it on, and of distributing it.

Filtering the lacquer

Before applying the undercoating, the lacquer is basically strained. When the tube of lacquer is first opened, there is no need to strain the lacquer. However, once the tube is opened, a small amount of dust difficult to see with the naked eye will get mixed in with the lacquer. If you paint a vessel with lacquer that has dust in it, bubbles will arise on the surface, and the finish will not be beautiful.

In order to remove the dust, it is necessary to filter the lacquer using filter paper.

Place the lacquer on the filter paper, pinch both ends of the paper with your fingers, and twist. If you twist hard enough, you can squeeze out clean lacquer from the filter paper.

4 下地塗り | Undercoating

中塗り

　錆漆の上に最初に黒漆を塗ることを「中塗り」と言います。

　まずテレピン油で希釈(きしゃく)した黒漆を白磁の小皿の縁(ふち)に置いて、皿の底に流れるスピードで漆の濃度をみます。漆の場合、その日の天候によって状態が変わるので、常に温度と湿度を気にかけます。これは45年間、漆芸修復をやっている私に染みついた習慣です。

　次に、面相筆を黒漆に浸す際は、筆の内部に漆を充填させるために必ず根元まで浸(ひた)します。筆内部は漆の燃料タンクのようなものです。

　中塗りの作業は絵を描くのではなく、錆漆の表面に漆の被膜(ひまく)を均等につけるような作業です。まず塗るべき箇所に漆を一定間隔で筆先から出して、ちょんちょんと置いていきます。そうして錆漆の上に均等に配られた漆を、次に筆先で全体に伸ばします。私が漆を「塗る」のではなく「置く」「配る」と表現するのはそのためです。割れなどの細く長い部分の塗りも、一気に長い線を引く必要はなく、漆を短い線を描くように数回に分けて置いていき、後でそれを伸ばして繋げます。

Middle coat

The first application of kuro-urushi on top of the sabi-urushi is called the nakanuri or "middle coat." First, kuro-urushi diluted with turpentine is placed on the rim of white porcelain dish. The density of the lacquer is measured by the speed at which it flows to the middle of the dish. Lacquer responds readily to the surrounding atmosphere, its condition changing depending on the weather of the day, so I always pay attention to the temperature and humidity. This is a habit now thoroughly ingrained in me after forty-five years of working as a lacquer art restorer.

When I dip a menso fude brush in kuro-urushi, I always dip it to the very base of the brush, so as to saturate the inside of the brush with lacquer. The inside of the brush is like a fuel tank for the lacquer.

Applying the middle coat is nothing like painting a picture. It is a process of very evenly distributing a film of lacquer upon the surface of the sabi-urushi. First of all, the lacquer is dabbed onto the sabi-urushi area carefully and at regular distancing with the tip of the brush. Next, the lacquer is spread evenly over the entire surface of the sabi-urushi. This is why I use the words "place" and "distribute" when describing this process.

When lacquering long and thin areas such as cracks, it is not necessary to draw a long line all at once. Place the lacquer in short lines several times, and later extend the lines to connect them.

The trick is to hold the brush with the thumb down and opposite the index and middle

4 下地塗り | Undercoating

　筆は親指を下にして人差し指と中指で挟んで持ち、塗る時に小指を器に当てて筆運びの支点にすることがコツです。小指が軸となって手を支えることで筆先が安定し、塗る際のぶれが少なくなります。中央部分に漆が塗れたら塗った漆をエッジまで伸ばして、際の部分を仕上げていきます。

　下地塗りの意味は、黒漆で錆漆をコーティングして防水の被膜をつくることです。際の部分は錆漆からはみ出すことのないよう、中央の漆を伸ばして仕上げていきます。ただし、漆を厚く塗りすぎることは避けます。漆が乾いた時に縮んでしまい、表面がしわになることがあるためです。

上塗り

　中塗りした黒漆が乾いたら、次に「上塗り」を行います。上塗りも同様に黒漆で行いますが、黒色の上に黒色を塗るのは難しいので、上塗りの際は色漆を少し混ぜ、色を違えて塗ります。漆は塗り重ねるごとに防水効果が増していきます。中塗りの1回だけでは黒漆の一部が錆漆に染み込んでしまい十分なコーティングができていない場合がありますが、2度塗りすることで、水使いに十分耐え、防水効果が持続する金継ぎに仕上がります。

fingers, and to place the little finger on the vessel as the fulcrum of the brush stroke. The tip of the brush is stabilized by the fulcrum action of the little finger. When the center part is coated with lacquer, we extend lacquer gradually to the edge, and then finish the edge.

The purpose of the base coating is to coat the sabi-urushi with kuro-urushi and thereby make a waterproof film on it. The edge of the lacquer is finished by extending the center of the lacquer so that it does not protrude from the sabi-urushi, but ends precisely and uniformly with it. We take care, for this reason, not to apply the lacquer too thickly, because the lacquer may shrink when it dries, causing the surface to wrinkle.

Top coating

After the middle coat of kuro-urushi is dry, the uwanuri or "top coat" is applied. However, it is difficult to paint black on black, so we mix a little colored urushi into the kuro-urushi to vary the color. The waterproofing effect of lacquer increases with each coat. By applying at least two coats of lacquer, it is possible to make kintsugi that can remain waterproof.

私の金継ぎ修復の工程 | My Kintsugi Restoration Process

5 装飾 | Decoration

装飾（金蒔き）

　下地塗りが終わったら、金継ぎのハイライトである「金蒔き」の工程に入ります。修復箇所の装飾で一般的なものは「金」ですが、他にも白金、銀、錫、螺鈿、金箔、色漆など多様な組み合わせがあります。器の模様を生かす「絵つなぎ」という技法もあります。本書では、金粉による一般的な装飾について説明します。

Decoration (Kin-maki)

Once the base coating is done, we can finally begin kin-maki, "sowing gold," the highlight of kintsugi. Gold is the most common material used to decorate mended areas, but there are many alternatives, including platinum, silver, tin, mother-of-pearl, gold leaf, and colored lacquer and these can be used in combination. There is also a technique called e-tsunagi, "picture connecting," which gives play to the design that already exists on the vessel. In this book, I will introduce the most common method of decoration, which emplays gold powder.

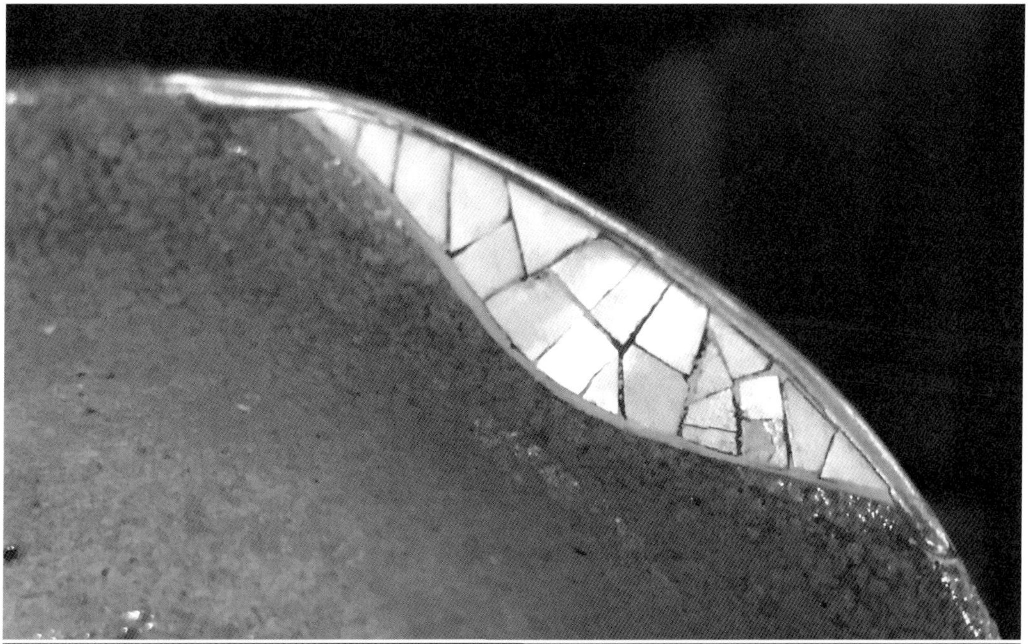

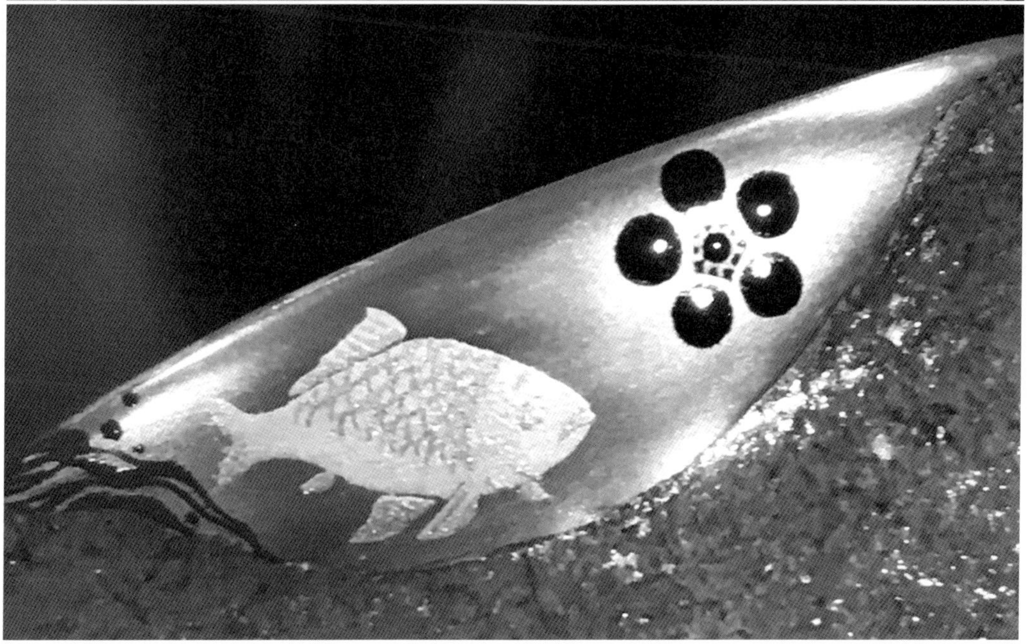

Chapter 4

5 装飾 | Decoration

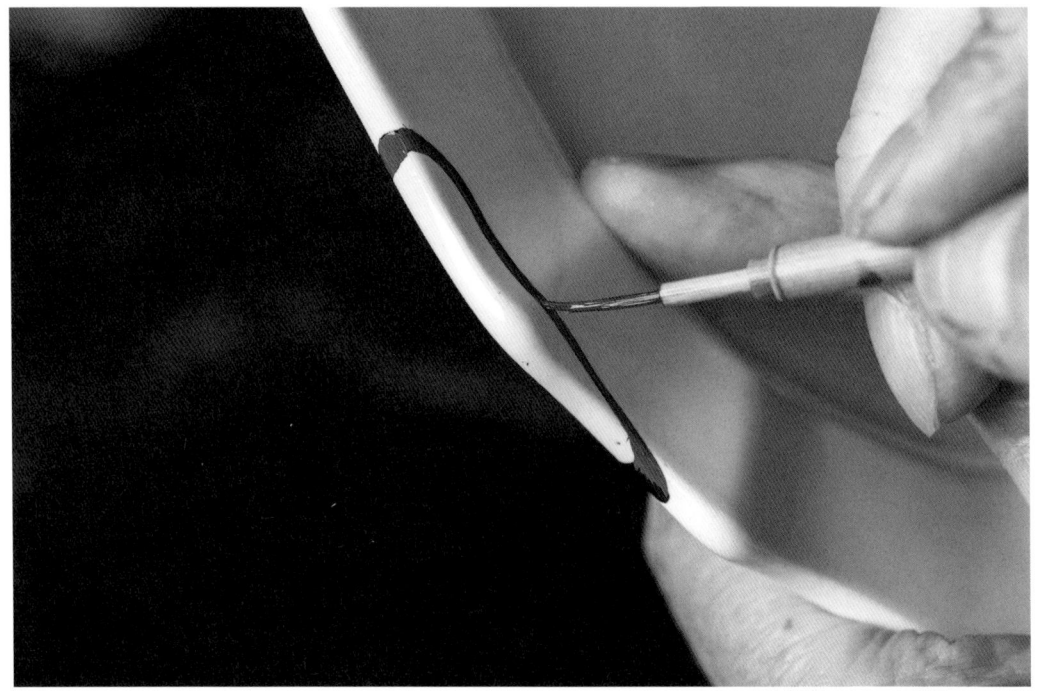

下絵用の弁柄漆を塗る

　下地塗りの上に直接金を蒔くのではなく、下絵用の漆・弁柄漆を塗る必要があります。2度塗りして防水効果を高めた黒漆の上に金を蒔いても問題なさそうに思えますし、そもそも数ある色漆の中でなぜ弁柄漆を塗るのでしょうか。

　それは、弁柄漆には鉱物から採れる酸化鉄を原料とする赤色顔料が入っているからです。生漆にも黒漆にも顔料は入っていません。赤色顔料の粒子は金の粒子をしっかり捉まえて、剝離しないように表面に金をキープしてくれることに加えて、赤色が金の発色を良くしてくれます。また、顔料の粒子の上に蒔かれることで、金の粒子は乱反射を起こして輝きを増します。弁柄漆は、最小の金で最大の効果をもたらす、金蒔きには最高の下絵漆なのです。

金蒔きのタイミング

　弁柄漆を乾燥させ、表面に薄い被膜ができたタイミングで、完全に凝固する前に金

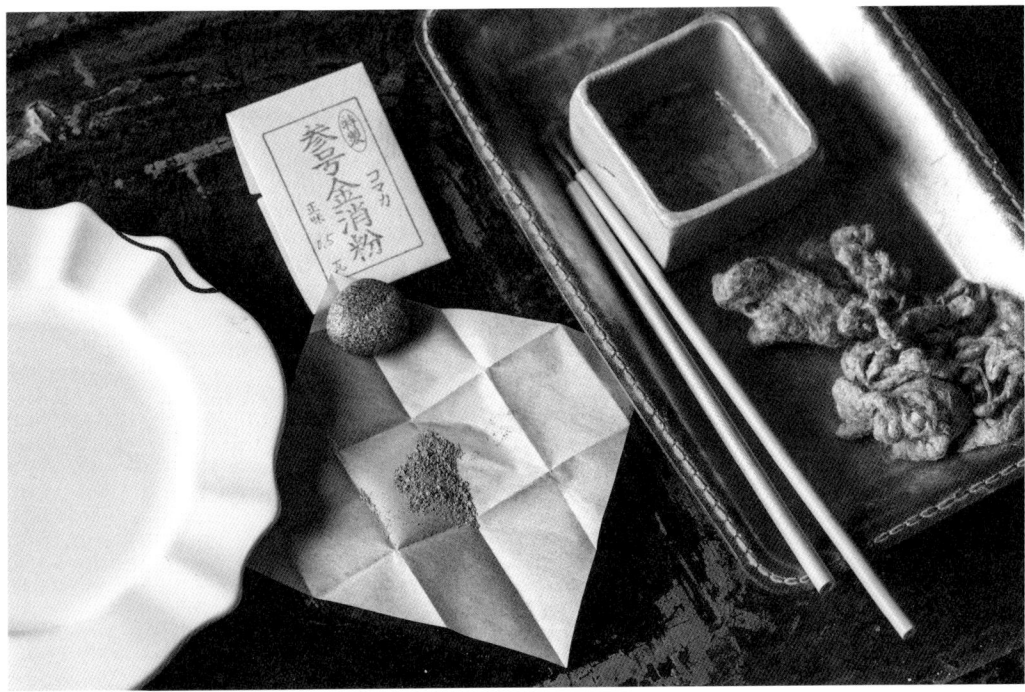

The bengara-urushi underpainting

Why do we apply bengara red iron oxide urushi before sowing the gold?

It would seem no problem to sow the gold directly onto the kuro-urushi, base coating. But instead, we first apply bengara-urushi. Neither raw lacquer nor kuro-urushi contain any pigment. Bengara-urushi contains red pigment made from mineral extract iron oxide. The particles of red pigment adhere to the gold particles and protect them on the surface, preventing them from being peeled off. The red color also enhances the color of the gold. Also, sown amidst the pigment particles, the gold particles create a diffuse reflection that increases their brilliance. Bengara-urushi is the best kind of lacquer for coating the surface onto which the gold will be sown. As it gives maximum effect from a minimum amount of gold.

The kin-maki timing

Kin-maki begins only after a thin film has formed on the surface of the bengara-urushi, and must be completed before the lacquer solidifies. If the lacquer is still too soft when the gold is sprinkled, the gold particles sink into it. The speed at which the lacquer dries depends

5 装飾 | Decoration

蒔きを行います。弁柄漆の乾きが甘く軟らかすぎると、金を蒔いた際に金の粒子が漆に沈み込んでしまい、発色が悪く、何度も蒔き直すことになります。また、弁柄漆が凝固してしまうと金が上手く載りません。弁柄漆が乾く速度はその日の気候によって異なりますが、私が思う金蒔きの最適なタイミングは、弁柄漆の塗面に息を吹きかけ、その息で塗面が少し曇ったようになった時です。

金蒔き

金蒔きは毛棒と真綿で行います。まず金粉を毛棒で掬い、毛棒の軸を人差し指でとんとん、と叩いて弁柄漆の表面に金を落とします。この時、作業机の上に必ず白い紙を敷きます。金粉はたくさん蒔いて良いですが、金は高価で貴重なので、器から落とした余分な金粉を白い紙で「見える化」して受け、その金を再利用します。

十分な量の金が弁柄漆の上に載ったら、真綿を摘むようにして持ち、金を優しくそっと磨きます。金の載せ方が不十分だと、真綿が弁柄漆に触れてしまい、微量な綿くずが漆に混じってしまいます。「金を磨く」というよりも、真綿の表面で「金を撫でる」と

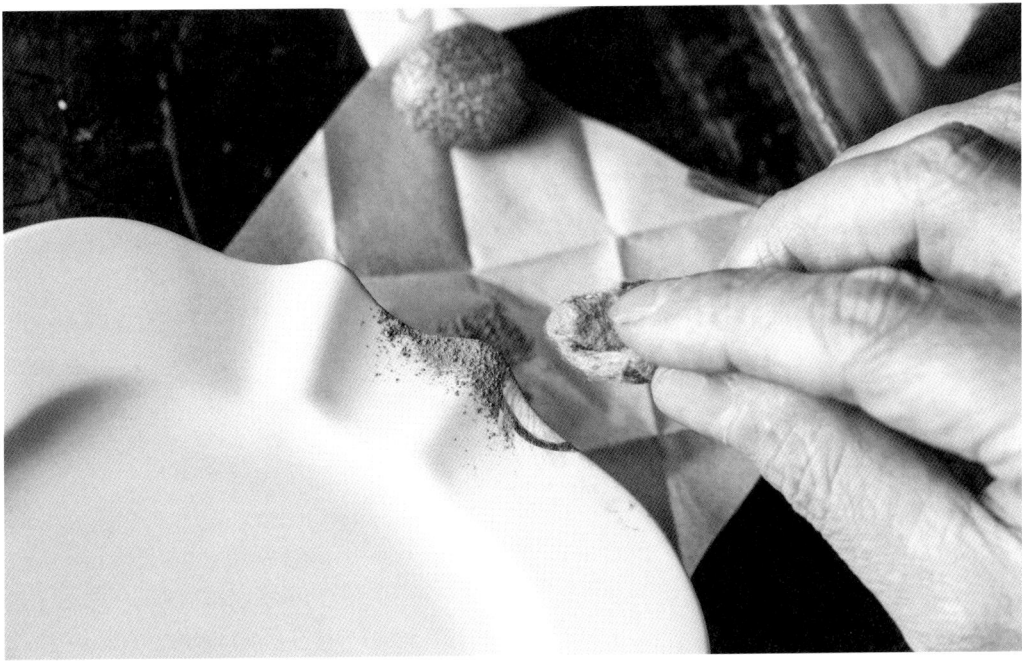

on the weather on the day of application. In my opinion, the best way to determine the timing for sowing the gold is to blow a little on the lacquered surface. When the timing is right, the surface will cloud slightly with your breath.

The kin-maki method

The sowing of the gold powder is done using a kebo brush and cotton. First, scoop up gold powder with the kebo and tap the shaft of the kebo with your index finger to sprinkle the gold onto the surface of the bengara-urushi. At this time, a piece of white paper should be placed on the work table. We can wind up sprinkling a lot of gold powder, and being generous with the gold sowing is fine, but gold is expensive and precious, so by using the white paper we can see and gather up the excess that has fallen onto it, and reuse it.

Once enough gold has been placed on the bengara-urushi, hold a piece of cotton as though pinching it lightly, and gently polish the surface of the gold. If the cotton happens to touch the bengara-urushi, a bit of it could get into the bengara-urushi. Rather than "polishing" the gold, a more appropriate image would be that you are "stroking" the gold with the surface of the cotton. If you gently move the cotton up and down without applying pressure, the gold will eventually start to shine. The cotton turns golden brown as it becomes soaked with gold powder. Such gold-soaked cotton is easier to work with. After the first sowing of gold,

5 装飾 | Decoration

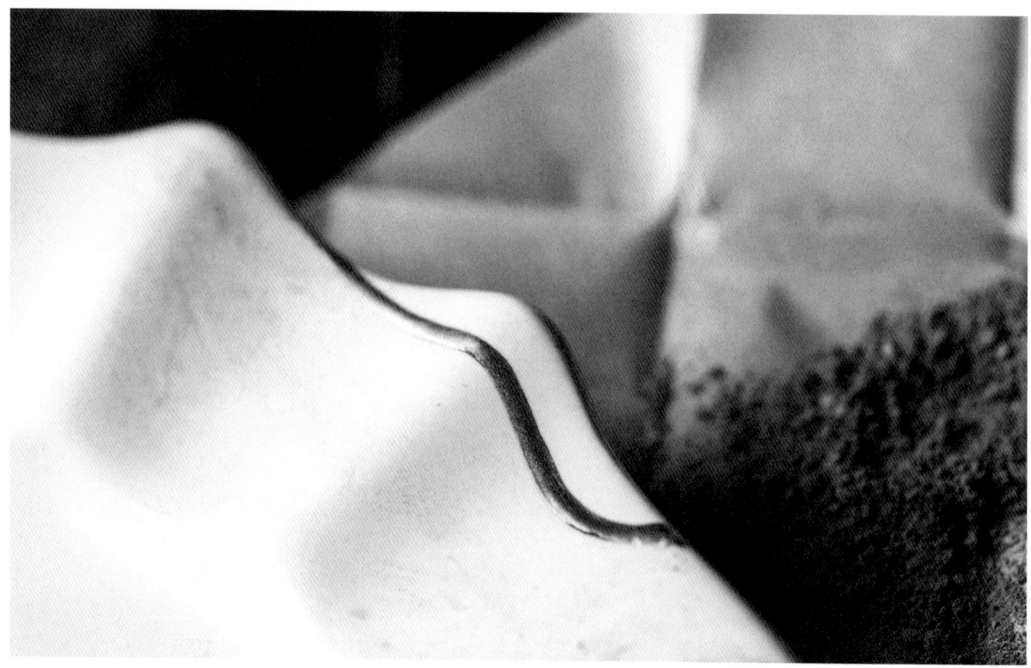

いうイメージに近いです。決して指圧を加えず、そっと真綿を上下させるとやがて金が輝きだします。真綿は使い込むと金粉がついて黄金色(こがねいろ)になりますが、金粉が滲みた真綿の方が作業はしやすいです。1回金蒔きをしたら、様子を見てもう1回行います。2回目は既に弁柄漆に金粉が載っているので、真綿に直接金粉をつけて、金蒔きを行っても構いません。

金について

本章では「金」または「金粉」と一語で言っていますが、実は金にも色々な種類があり、私は修復する器の個性と修復のデザインによって使い分けています。最も多く使う金粉は、「参号(さんごう)消し粉(ふん)」と呼ばれるもので、柔らかくきめ細かな金の輝きを楽しめます。

参号消し粉より粒子の大きな「丸粉(まるふん)」という金粉は、金蒔き後に研ぎ上げることで、金属的で鋭利(えいり)な輝きを放ちます。金粉以外での金の装飾には「金箔貼り」があり、厚さ1万分の2ミリという薄さの箔を膠(にかわ)で貼り付けることで、面全体を金色にします。

if a second sowing is required, it can be done directly using the cotton.

About gold

For the sake of simplicity, I have used the words "gold" or "gold powder" throughout this chapter, but in fact there are many kinds of gold, and I use different kinds depending on the personality of the vessel to be restored and the design of the mending. The gold powder I use most often is called Sango Keshifun, "Gold Powder No. 3," which gives a fine, soft golden shine.

Marufun "round powder," which has larger particles than the Sango Keshifun, gives a bright and metallic shine when polished. Another way to decorate the mended area is to use gold leaf, which can be as thin as two-ten-thousandths of a millimeter. Nikawa animal glue is used to apply it.

私の金継ぎ修復の工程 | My Kintsugi Restoration Process

6 粉固め(ふんがた) | Powder cementing

粉固め(生漆どめ)

　金蒔きした器を室で数日間かけて乾かした後、金蒔きの表面に適度に希釈した生漆を塗り、少し時間をおいてから拭き取ります。この作業を「粉固め(生漆どめ)」と言います。金と弁柄漆の顔料のすき間に漆が入り込んで金の付着がより強固になり、長期間の使用に耐えられるようになるのです。ただし、拭き取らずにいると、漆が硬化して表面が黒ずんでしまうので注意が必要です。

　粉固めの後、器を室で5日から1週間ほど乾燥させると金継ぎ修復は完成ですが、1か月ほど、水洗いは控えるように勧めています。

　自然素材のみで行う金継ぎ修復は時間がかかりますが、合成接着剤の修復よりはるかに丈夫で長持ちします。また、合成接着剤や化学塗料は器の地(いた)を傷めてしまう場合がありますが、自然素材の漆は強固な接着力と防水性で器の地を守ります。神社仏閣の修復で古い漆を落としてみると、内部の木が傷まずに残っていることからも、漆が木を守り続けてきたことが分かります。

Powder cementing (Raw lacquer coating)

After drying the gold-decorated vessel in the muro for several days, moderately diluted raw lacquer is applied to the surface of the gold. The lacquer penetrates into the gaps between the gold and the bengara-urushi pigment, making the gold adhere more firmly to the surface and increasing its durability. In this process, we have to wipe off the raw lacquer only a short time after application. If not wiped off, the lacquer will harden and the surface will turn black.

After the powder cementing process, the vessel is placed in the muro to dry for five days to a week, and that completes the kintsugi restoration. It is recommended to refrain from washing the vessel with water for about a month.

Restoring with kintsugi using only natural materials takes more time, but results in a much stronger and longer-lasting restoration than repairing with synthetic adhesives. In addition, synthetic adhesives and chemical paints can damage the original vessel, while natural lacquer protects the base material of the vessel with its strong adhesive and waterproofing properties. When old lacquer is removed from restored shrines and temples, the wood inside remains undamaged, demonstrating that the lacquer has been protecting the wood.

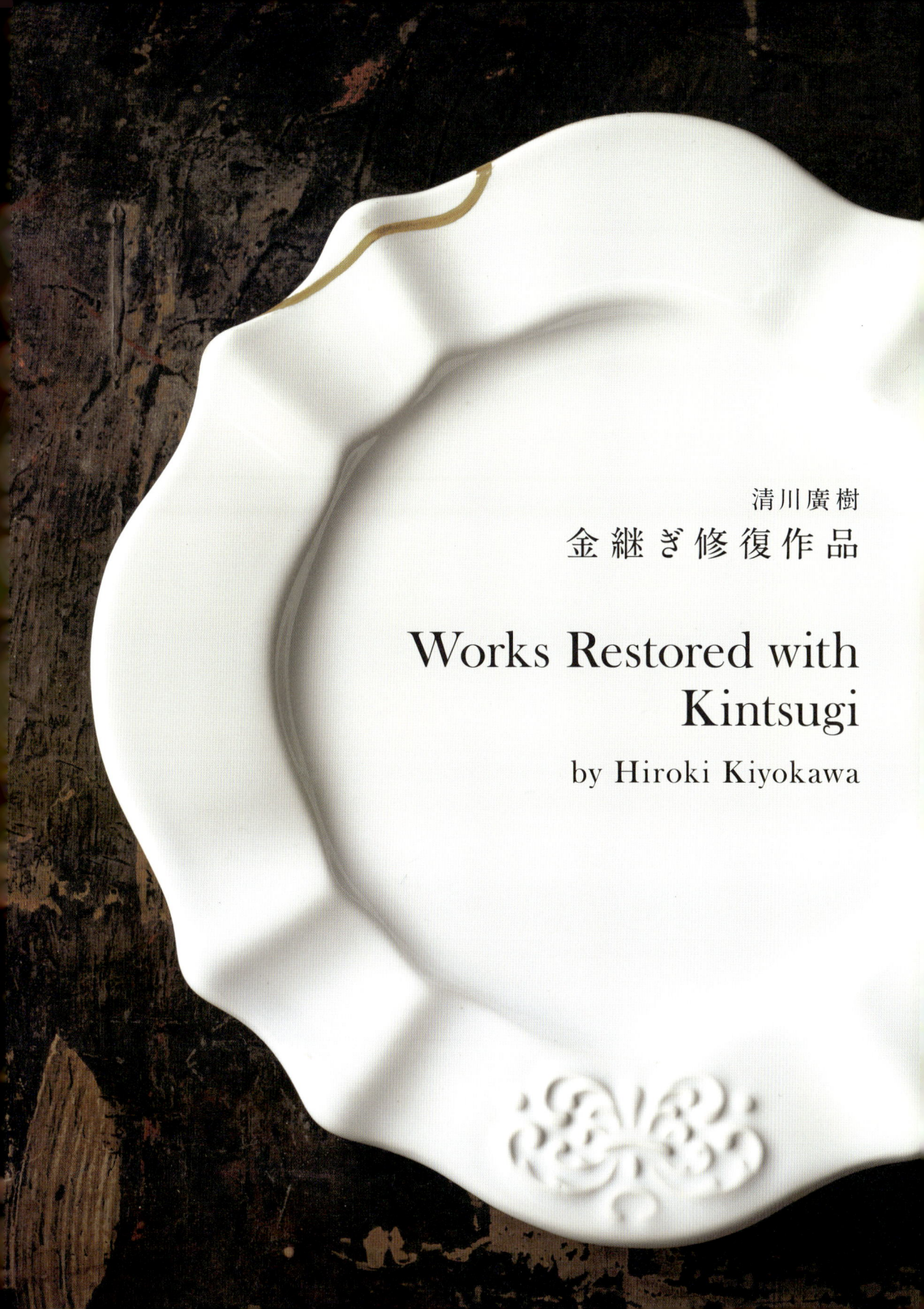

清川廣樹
金継ぎ修復作品

Works Restored with Kintsugi

by Hiroki Kiyokawa

清川廣樹 金継ぎ修復作品 | Restored with Kintsugi by Hiroki Kiyokawa

黒筒茶碗

　筒茶碗の扱いとして、冬の時期には茶を点てて客にすすめるには茶碗がほどよく温くなくてはならず、そのために茶碗の形状も湯が冷めにくい筒状になっているそうです。

　私は黒い器に縦に入ったひびを冬の夜空に輝く一瞬の閃光（せんこう）に見立て、鋭利な輝きを持つ金でデザインをしました。「冬の雷（らい）」は俳句の季語にもなっていて、大気が不安定になって発生することから「雪起こし雷」とも言われています。冬季にこの茶碗を手に取った方が、暖かいお茶を飲みながら、雪を呼ぶ雷を思い浮かべてもらえたらと思います。

Black Cylindrical Tea Bowl

Cylindrical tea bowls are used to make tea and serve it to guests in the winter season, because their tall and narrow shape prevents the water and the tea from getting cold.

My kintsugi design for this black bowl was to liken its vertical crack to a flash of lightning in the winter night sky, and to utilize a gold that has a sharp sparkle. "Winter thunder" is a seasonal expression in haiku, and is also called "snow-causing thunder" because it occurs when the atmosphere becomes unstable. I hope that those who hold this tea bowl in their hands during the winter season may, as they drink warm tea from it, think of the thunder that brings snow.

黒楽茶碗

　楽焼ならではの男性的な器のフォルムに合わせ、器に入った大きなひびを山脈に見立てて、大胆な金継ぎデザインを考えました。光が当たる加減で、金が器の表面に山脈のように浮かび上がるイメージです。さらに、ひびの走りから夜空に閃く稲妻を連想し、仕上がりはよりダイナミックになりました。

Black Raku Tea Bowl

In order to match the masculine form of Raku ware, I came up with a bold kintsugi design which makes the cracks look like a mountain range. My image was that, depending on how the light hit it, the gold would loom up like a mountain range. The streaks also make one think of a lightning bolt flashing in the night sky, effectively making the outcome all-the-more more dynamic.

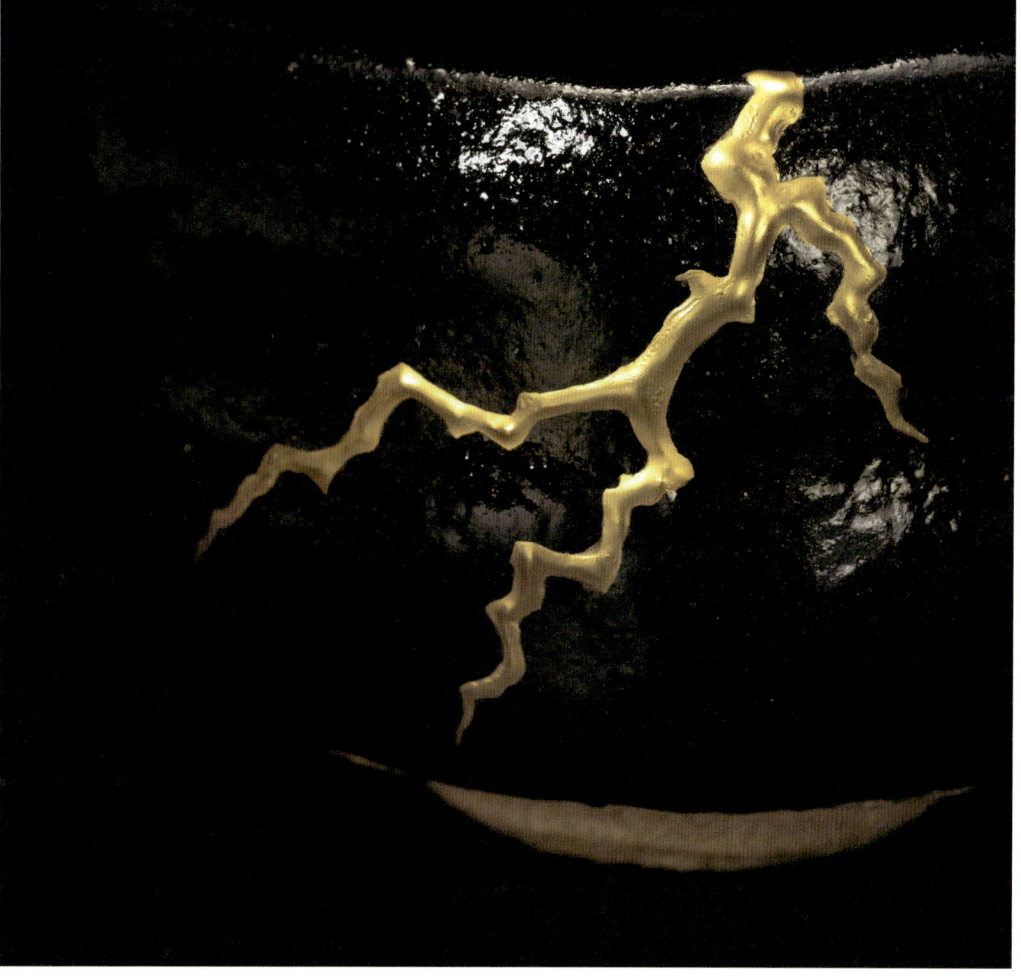

清川廣樹 金継ぎ修復作品 | Restored with Kintsugi by Hiroki Kiyokawa

赤茶碗

　この茶碗は江戸時代前期の茶人で久田家3代・久田宗全が箱書したもので、箱にはシンプルに「赤茶碗」と書かれています。宗全は楽茶碗や花入といた茶道具の作陶を得意としたそうで、宗全が手づくねの赤茶碗の修復を依頼されたことは私にとって大変光栄なことでした。
　経年により発生した貫入(かんにゅう)の味わいが引き立つように、柔らかな金色で割れを継ぎ、さらに弁柄漆と合わせることで器の色との調和を図(はか)り、赤茶碗の名に恥じないように修復させていただきました。

Red Tea Bowl

The box for this tea bowl was inscribed simply "red tea bowl" by Hisada Sozen, a tea master of the Edo period and the third generation of the Hisada family. Sozen is said to have been good at handcrafting tea ceramics such as Raku bowls and flower vases. It was a great honor for me to be asked to restore the red tea bowl that Sozen had made.
 In order to bring out the taste of the kannyu crackling caused by the passage of time, I joined the cracks with soft gold color, and furthermore, by combining it with bengara-urushi, I aimed to harmonize it with the color of the bowl and thereby restore the bowl in a way that honored its name, "red tea bowl."

飴釉茶碗

　飴釉は窯の中で焼きあがると褐色になる釉薬です。光が当たると複雑な色調となり、発色の濃いところは吸い込まれるような単色で、その周りや発色の薄いところは様々な色が混ざり合っています。

　この器には、金粉の代わりに銀粉を蒔き、朱合漆（植物性の油を適宜加えて精製される光沢のある飴色の漆）で上塗りする白檀塗の技法が合うと考えました。朱合漆を塗ることで銀粉は飴色に変化し、器に溶け込んでいきます。また、白檀塗は器を手に取った時、手の肌色と飴色が美しく調和して、さらに深い味わいを持ちます。

Ameyu Tea Bowl

Ameyu is a glaze that turns brown when fired in the kiln. It becomes a complex color tone when it is exposed to light, with the darker areas being a deep monochromatic color, and the surrounding areas and lighter areas being a mixture of various colors.

　I used silver rather than gold powder and employed the byakudan-nuri "sandalwood application" technique in which the silver was topped with a finishing coat of lustrous amber-colored shuai lacquer. By applying shuai lacquer, the silver powder changed to an amber color and blended into the vessel. In addition, byakudan-nuri provides a more subtle pleasure when you hold it in your hand, as the skin color of your hand and the amber color harmonize beautifully.

清川廣樹 金継ぎ修復作品 ｜ Works Restored with Kintsugi by Hiroki Kiyokawa

備前鶴首花入

　備前焼は、良質な陶土で成形、乾燥させた後、絵付けもせず釉薬も使わずそのまま焼いた土味がよく表れている焼き物です。もともと古墳時代の製法が次第に変化したもので、平安時代に生活用器の碗、皿、盤や瓦などが生産されたのがその始まりといわれています。素朴で荒々しい備前焼は器の風合いが自然そのもので、通常の金継ぎでは金が負けてしまうため、その一部を黒漆で縁取りすることで、金を際立たせるようにしました。

Bizen Flower Vase

Bizen ware is a type of pottery that is made of high-quality clay, dried, and fired without decoration or glaze. It gradually evolved out of pottery techniques used in the prehistoric Kofun period, and is said to have originated in the Heian period (794–1185), with the production of bowls, plates, boards, and roof tiles. Bizen pottery is simple and rough, and the texture of the ware is so natural that the gold would be overpowered if I used the usual style of kintsugi, so I made the gold stand out by framing part of it with black lacquer.

古上野釉元窯花入

　釉薬の穏やかな色合いが印象的で、素朴な味わいながら優美な佇(たたず)まいを持つ花入です。聞くところによると、作家は長年九州で活動した後、近年はアメリカのボストンに活動拠点を移し、前衛的な作品にも取り組んでいるようです。一般的な金継ぎでは作家の個性を生かせないため、私なりに修復のテーマをつくりました。花入に縦に生じたひびを「数珠(じゅず)」に、釉薬のうねりを「世の移ろい」に見立てて金継ぎをデザインし、数珠をモチーフにすることで、出会いと結びつきの大切さを表現しました。

Old AganoFlower Vase

The gentle color of the glaze is impressive, and this flower vase has a simple yet graceful appearance. I hear that the artist was active in Kyushu for many years, but recently moved to Boston in the U.S. and has been working on avant-garde works. Since I would not be able to give life to the artist's individuality if I did the kintsugi in the standard style, I created my own theme for it. I designed the kintsugi using the vertical crack in the vase as a string of prayer beads, and the undulations of the glaze as the changes of the world. By using the beads as a motif, I expressed the importance of encounters and connections.

清川廣樹 金継ぎ修復作品 | Works Restored with Kintsugi by Hiroki Kiyokawa

アンティーク切子ワイングラス
東ドイツ

　透き通った海の色を思わせるブルーのグラスを見ながら、海底に眠る宝箱のような密やかな輝きを持つ金色での繕いを想像しました。切子の装飾を邪魔をしないさり気ない金が、このグラスの修復に相応しいと考えました。2箇所の口欠けを2滴の雫のようなかたちに修復して柔らかな色目の金を蒔き、グラスから雫が今にもこぼれ落ちようとする様を表現しています。

Antique Kiriko Wine Glass
East Germany

As I looked at the blue glass, which reminded me of the color of the crystal clear sea, I thought about restoring it with a gold that has a subtle glow like a treasure chest lying at the bottom of the sea. I thought that this gold, with its subdued color that would complement the faceted kiriko decoration, would be appropriate for the restoration of this wine glass. I repaired the two chips on the rim in the shape of two drops and decorated them with the soft colored gold. I tried to express that the drops are about to spill out of the wine glass.

ガラス花器
岩田久利作

　モノトーン基調の大胆なデザインながら優美なフォルムの花器です。独特な存在感があり、花器というよりもオブジェ(置物)としても楽しめる作品です。黒い縁にある欠けは金で繕うよりもメタリックな輝きの白金が相応しく、継ぎのラインを少し歪めることで、花器の持つ個性に寄り添えると考え、楕円状の白金のリングを欠け部分にデザインしました。

Glass Vase
by Hisatoshi Iwata

This vase has a bold monotone design and a graceful shape. It has a unique presence, and is one of those pieces that you would rather enjoy as an object than as a vase. Rather than using gold to mend the chip on the black rim, metallic shining platinum was more appropriate, and I thought that it would match the vase's character better if the line of the chip were somewhat bent, so I made it into an oblong ring design.

清川廣樹 金継ぎ修復作品 | Works Restored with Kintsugi by Hiroki Kiyokawa

白釉中皿

　普段使いの四角い中皿の角が欠けて失われていました。まず漆に砥の粉（山の土）や和紙を混ぜて欠け部分を接着させ、黒漆で二度塗りした後に螺鈿を蒔き、研ぎ上げました。漆黒の中に螺鈿の輝きが浮かび上がったところで、螺鈿の間に弁柄漆で下絵を描いて金蒔きして磨き上げ、モザイクのように仕上げました。ヨーロッパの教会の天井画とステンドグラスを思い浮かべ、何の変哲もない白い中皿に新しい景色をつくりました。

White Pottery Medium Dish

The corner of a medium-size rectangular dish for daily use was chipped and lost. First, I recreated the chipped part by mixing powdered clay and Japanese paper with urushi, then painted it twice with kuro-urushi, sprinkled mother-of-pearl onto it and polished it. When the brilliance of the mother-of-pearl emerged in the jet-black color, I drew underdrawings between the mother-of-pearl in bengara-urushi, sowed gold onto that and polished everythings to create a mosaic-like finished. Imagining the ceiling paintings and stained glass in European churches, I created a new landscape on a plain white plate.

白磁ミルクピッチャーとシュガーポット

　母が愛用していたミルクピッチャーとシュガーポットの縁欠けを、器の白色に合うように柔らかな金で繕いました。縁の波型のデザインに合わせて金を蒔きましたが、ミルクピッチャーの持ち手とシュガーポットの蓋の摘みにも金のアクセントを入れて、白色の器の上に優しかった母の微笑みを金で表現してみました。この食器はありふれたものですが、私にとっては母の思い出が詰まった大事なもので、長く手元に置きたいと思っています。

White Porcelain Milk Pitcher and Sugar Pot

I repaired on the chipped rims of my mother's favorite milk pitcher and sugar pot with soft gold to match the white color of the vessels. I sprinkled gold to match the wavy design of the rim, but I also added gold accents to the handle of the milk pitcher and the knob of the sugar pot lid to express my mother's gentle smile on the white tableware. The two pieces of tableware are commonplace, but they are important to me because they are filled with memories of my mother, and I want to keep them for a long time.

特別対談 | A conversation between

人を繋ぐ名もなき茶碗
Connecting through the Enigma of a Kitchen Bowl

瀬川日照 | **Nissho Segawa**
本法寺 貫首 | abbot of Honpoji Temple

清川廣樹 | **Hiroki Kiyokawa**
修復師 | traditional restorer

叡昌山本法寺は、室町時代に活躍した日蓮宗僧侶、久遠成院日親上人（1407-88）によって築かれた日蓮宗の本山です。同寺には本阿弥光悦や長谷川等伯による作品が所蔵されています。

本作は、本法寺の台所用の茶碗として、長きにわたり使われてきました。庭園「巴の庭」（本阿弥光悦作）をイメージして金継ぎを施しております。本法寺の瀬川日照貫首より、寺宝として保管していただけることになりました。

修復した茶碗を納めた数か月後、その後の様子をお聞きするため本法寺をお訪ねしたところ、瀬川貫首にお迎えいただき、汲み出し茶碗をめぐるお話を伺うことができました。

Eihosan Honpoji is the head temple of the Nichiren sect of Buddhism and was founded by the Nichiren priest Kuon Seiin Nisshin (1407–88), who was active in the Muromachi period. The temple has a collection of works by Hon'ami Koetsu and Hasegawa Tohaku.

This kumidashi bowl had a long history as a bowl for kitchen use at Honpoji. Kintsugi was applied to it in the image of the temple's "Tomoe Garden" (designed by Hon'ami Koetsu). The abbot of Honpoji, Nissho Segawa, agreed to maintain the bowl as a temple treasure.

A few months after delivering the restored bowl, I visited Honpoji to inquire about the condition of the restoration. I was welcomed by Abbot Segawa, and able to hear the story about this kumidashi bowl.

本法寺　汲み出し茶碗

昭和時代
本山　本法寺蔵

Honpoji Kumidashi Bowl
Showa period (1926–1950)
Honpoji Temple

157

日の目を見た茶碗

瀬川　2017年の12月頃、探し物ついでに台所の縁の下の物置を整理していましたところ、一番奥から「本法寺台所」と書かれたこの茶碗がでてきました。見つけたけれども割れていて、特に口造りのところは欠けがひどかった。どうしようもないけど、もったいないなあと思いながら、ひとまず台所に置いていました。その次の日、たまたま清川さんが来訪されて、修復のお仕事をされているとお聞きしたので、この茶碗をお見せしたのです。

清川　本当に偶然でしたね。私はその日、貫首様のお知り合いの方と開山堂の葺き替えた昔の瓦を拝見するために伺っていました。その役割を終え傷んだ瓦の一枚に金継ぎを施し、長く保存していただきたいと思っていたのですが……まさか先にお茶碗の修復に携わることになろうとは(笑)。

瀬川　見つけた時は直そうとも思いませんでしたし、本来なら捨てているはずのお茶碗ですからね。まるで導かれたような気持ちになりました。清川さんにお会いして、「これは"ご縁"だ」と思いましたよ。

A Bowl is Reborn

Segawa: Around December of 2017, I was sorting out the storage space under the temple kitchen while looking for something. Amidst the various forgotten objects I came upon this bowl with the words "Honpoji kitchen" inscribed on it. The bowl was cracked, with especially bad chipping at the lip. It seemed a hopeless case, but I thought it was a waste to just have it lying around forgotten somewhere, so I decided to put it in the kitchen for a while. The very next day, you visited me and I learned that you did restoration work, so I showed you the bowl.

Kiyokawa: That was a remarkable coincidence. On that day, I was visiting with an acquaintance of yours to see the old roof tiles that had been replaced at the Kaizando, the Founder's Hall. Those slate tiles had protected the hall for many years, and I was hoping to mend one of them with kintsugi, so that it might be preserved and commemorated. I never imagined that before the tile project would begin, I would first be charged with restoring this forgotten bowl [laughter].

162　特別対談 ── 人を繋ぐ名もなき茶碗

清川　12月末くらいにお預かりして、半年くらいかけて修復しました。仕上がりに関しては一任していただいておりましたので、元の姿をできるだけ残しつつ、本法寺様ならではの何かしらの要素を入れたいなと思いながらイメージを膨らませていきました。そして、日蓮宗の題目「南無妙法蓮華経」を髭のように伸ばして書いた「髭題目」と、本阿弥光悦が残した「巴の庭」の枯山水の滝の水滴をイメージした金継ぎをしました。金だけですと器と同系色になるので、メリハリを出すために白金も施して仕上げました。

瀬川　戻ってきた時、「よくここまで直ったなあ」とただただ感心しました。まさか縁の下で見つけた茶碗がこんなにきれいに立派になって戻ってくるなんてね。清川さんのおかげで、本当に嬉しいです。

Segawa: When I found the bowl, I didn't even think of fixing it, and left to my own devices, eventually I would have thrown it away. I felt as if I was guided. When I met you, I thought, "This is karma."

Kiyokawa: I received the bowl around the end of December, and worked on it over the next six months. The design of the restoration was left up to me. I felt it was important to keep as much of the original appearance as possible, but I also wanted to add some elements unique to Honpoji Temple. Details of two artistic compositions within the temple provided inspiration. First was the very unique calligraphy of the refuge mantra of the Nichiren sect, Nam-Myoho-Renge-Kyo "Homage to the Lotus Sutra of the Supreme Dharma." This famous calligraphy composition has acquired the name "Hige-daimoku" for the long whisker-like filaments which extend outward from the kanji. The second source of inspiration for me was the waterfall of the karesansui rock garden at the temple; the famous Tomoe Garden composed by Hon'ami Koetsu. I wanted to recreate the impression of the water droplets springing from the waterfall. If I used only gold, the mending would be the same color as the vessel, so I also applied platinum, to give it variation.

Segawa: When I got the bowl back, I was just amazed at how well it had been restored. I had no idea that the little orphan vessel that I found forgotten under the kitchen would come back so splendid and beautiful. Thanks to you, I am really happy.

名もなき茶碗の新発見

瀬川　発見当時、この茶碗について分かることは胴部に書いてある「本法寺台所」「有志」「清水三谷口」のみで乏しいものでした。せっかく日の目を見たのだから、と愛着が湧いてきて、誰が、どこで、どんな用途で使っていたのか知りたくなりましたね。

　ある時、茶道資料館の学芸員の方に茶碗をお見せしたところ、作陶したのが清水焼の谷口さんという陶芸家だと分かったので、連絡をして、実際に見ていただいたんです。

　そして、作られたのは昭和23年（1948）で、作者は当代谷口正典氏のお父様である谷口良三氏であるということが分かりました。

　「有志」は谷口氏からご寄付いただいたことを示しており、「清水三谷口」はご自身のサインといったところでしょうか。「本法寺台所」はそのままの意味で、台所用で日用雑器として使われていたのではないかと思います。

　本法寺は利休居士にゆかりがあることやかつて茶道研修所の寮にもなっていたことから、やはり茶道との関係があるのではないかなと考えておりますが……。

A Recovered History

Segawa: At the time of its discovery, the only thing that could be known about this bowl was that it had the words "Honpoji kitchen," "supporter," and "Kiyomizu San Taniguchi" written on it. Because of its fortuitous discovery and restoration, I became attached to the bowl, and I wanted to know who used it, where, and for what purpose.

　One day, when I showed it to a curator at the Chado Research Center, he told me that it was likely made by a Kiyomizu-ware potter named Taniguchi, so I decided to seek him out and ask about the bowl in person. I found out that the bowl was made in 1948 and that the potter was Mr. Ryozo Taniguchi, the father of the present-generation family head, Masanori Taniguchi.

　The "supporter" indicates that the bowl was donated to the temple by Mr. Taniguchi, and the "Kiyomizu San Taniguchi" was his signature. The words "Honpoji kitchen" mean just that. It was probably used in the kitchen as an everyday item. Since Honpoji is associated with Rikyu and was once a dormitory for a chado training institute, I think the bowl may have some connection with chado.

Connecting through the Enigma of a Tea Bowl 165

清川 「台所」というのが興味深いです。お茶を飲む茶碗としてはもちろん、ある時には水指、またある時には茶筅を洗う時に使ったり、時にはお酒を注いでいたかもしれませんね。はっきりしないからこそ、想像が膨らむ。きっといろんな用途で使われてきたのでしょう。

瀬川 胴部の字も"あじ"のある枯れた字で素晴らしいです。こんな風に気軽に書かれているのを見ると台所用なんだろうと納得してしまいますね。

大出世した茶碗

清川 東京での催事でこのお茶碗を展示させていただいた際、これを見るために列ができるほど多くの方が興味を持っておられました。「大きさも金継ぎも立派ですね」とのお声をいただきながらご所蔵先の本法寺や陶芸家についてお調べになったりして、この茶碗をきっかけにして色々なことに関心を持っていただけるのは嬉しいですね。私自身、「日常で活躍していた器が時代を超えて、再び新たな時代を生きて欲しい」と気持ちを込めていますから。

瀬川 本当に大出世した茶碗です。修復されてからわずか1年くらいの間にいろんな人の目に触れてきました。きれいになっただけではなく、茶碗の由緒も分かって。この茶碗が本法寺に来た時からこうなる運命だったのでしょうかね。

清川 修復の仕事は人と人とを繋ぐことができるものだと強く実感します。こうして直すことで喜んでくれる方がいらっしゃるのは本当に嬉しいです。

瀬川 「壊れたけど、直したい」というものはおそらくどんな家にもあるのだと思います。色々な事情があるかもしれませんが、一度直したいと思ったならば、やはり「直した方が良いですよ」と勧めます。その器の価値は持ち主にしか分からないので自身のお気持ちが何より大切ですが、こうした不思議なご縁が待っているかもしれません。きっと器自身も喜んでいる、そんな気がしています。

Kiyokawa: The word "kitchen" is interesting here. It may have been used not only as a bowl for drinking tea, but also as a mizusashi or "water container" at times, or for washing the tea whisk, or even for pouring sake. The fact that it is not clear makes my imagination soar. It must have been used for various purposes.

Segawa: The reserved and tastefully understated handwriting on the side of the bowl is also wonderful. Seeing how it is written in such a casual way, I am convinced that this bowl was used in the kitchen.

A Happy Success

Kiyokawa: When I exhibited this tea bowl at an event in Tokyo, so many people were interested that there was a line to see it. I was happy that this little bowl from Honpoji could inspire curiosity in people, who would later look up the history of the temple and the potter who made it. I received compliments from many visitors, who praised the scale and design of the kintsugi as "magnificent." I was so happy to hear that, because I myself really put my heart into it. I hope that, like this piece of pottery, objects used in daily life can transcend the times and live again in a new era.

Segawa: This little bowl has really come a long way. It has been seen by so many people in just the year since it was restored. Not only has it been restored, but the history of the bowl has also been rediscovered. I can't help wondering if this bowl was destined for this trajectory from the time it came to Honpoji.

Kiyokawa: I strongly feel that the work of restoration can connect people to people. I feel very gratified to know that there are people who are happy with my work.

Segawa: I think every house has something broken which needs fixing. There may be various reasons, but once they want to fix it, I recommend that they do so. Only the owner knows the value of the vessel, so the owner's own feelings are most important, but there may be a mysterious connection waiting for that person. I have a feeling that the veseel itself will be happy.

おわりに

45年間の職人人生の中で、私が心がけている二つの言葉があります。
ひとつは「日々一生」、もうひとつは「労して苦せず」です。

「日々一生」

　修復品や金継ぎする器は、どれもご縁があって私のもとに来たものです。また、寺院修復など大がかりな現場では、多くの職人に作業を振り分けて仕事をしますが、色々な分野の職人との出会いもまた、ご縁があってのことです。

　修復には漆を使いますが、漆はその日の湿度、温度によって異なる変化をする"生き物"のような塗料です。漆は嘘をつかない正直な塗料で、職人が丁寧に扱うと他の塗料では出せない美しい輝きや色目を出して素材を守ってくれますが、良い漆でも雑に扱ってしまうと、それなりの仕上がりにしかなりません。ひとたび仕事が始まると、最善の修復を行うために、私は漆をその日の最高の状態に整え、一瞬一瞬、後戻りできない勝負の時に入ります。

　漆が嘘をつかないように、人間もまた、周りに自分を取り繕う(つくろ)ことができても、自分自身に嘘はつけず、自分の生き様は自分次第で決まります。私はこれまでの人生や、その時々の想いに嘘をつかず、できるだけ自分自身を深く見つめて、生き様が色濃く現れるような仕事をしたいと思っています。言い換えれば、漆に対して生き様を見せる覚悟で向き合わないと、漆は私に応えてくれないということです。

　私にとっての「日々一生」とは、二度とないかもしれない大切なご縁の機会を逃さないこと、また、最善の修復を行うための一瞬の判断を逃さず、漆と共に刻一刻、一日一日を積み重ね、先人たちが伝えてくれた伝統技法を後世に残せるように心がけることです。

Afterword

In the forty-five years of my life as a craftsman, there are two phrases that I have kept in mind: "Live every day as a lifetime" and "Work hard and suffer no pain."

Live every day as a lifetime

The various restored items and vessels that I work on have come to me through the profound motions of fate and fortune. In the case of large-scale projects such as temple restoration, the work is divided among many craftsmen. The encounter with craftsmen from various fields is also a result of fate.

We use lacquer for restoration. It is a kind of "living" paint that changes according to the humidity and temperature of the given day. Lacquer is an honest paint that does not lie, and if a craftsman handles it with care, it will produce a beautiful shine and color that no other paint can produce. I prepare the lacquer in the ideal and appropriate conditions for the day, in order to make the best restoration possible, and once the work begins, every moment is a moment of no return.

Just as lacquer does not lie, we human beings cannot lie to ourselves. Even if we can partially adapt and "mend" ourselves around others, our lives are ultimately determined by the dictates of our inner selves. I try to look within myself as deeply as possible and do my work in such a way that my life is deeply expressed. In other words, unless I am prepared to show my life to the lacquer, the lacquer will not respond to me.

For me, "Live every day as a lifetime" means to never miss an opportunity for an important encounter that may never happen again. Furthermore, it means to never miss a moment to make the best decision for restoration; To live each moment and each day with my chosen tradition to the fullest; To be mindful of the traditional techniques handed down by my predecessors; and to wholeheartedly convey that tradition to the future generation.

おわりに

「労して苦せず」

　「若い頃の苦労は買ってでもしなさい」とはよく言われる言葉です。実際、私の10代、20代の修業時代は、師匠から技術承継を受けるにあたり、厳しいことの連続でした。しかし、今になってようやく、なぜ師匠が自分に辛く当たったのか、分かってきました。師匠は私に叩き込んでくれたのです。身をもって覚えた技術は職人にとって血肉であり、「生きること」そのものであることを。修業時代の経験は、私にとってかけがえのない財産となりました。

　その上で今、私が思うのは、自分のとって大切なことであれば、たとえ無償であっても厭わず「労」に取り組もう、自分の糧になるのであれば、大変な「労」であっても「苦労」ではないのだ、ということです。逆に良い報酬をいただいても、自分の技法や時間を切り売りするような仕事であれば、それは「苦」以外の何物でもなく、そういったご依頼はお断りしよう、と思っています。

　今、私には大きな目標があります。それは衰退する日本の伝統工芸の現状を多くの人たちに理解していただき、その技術が後世に引き継がれるようにすることです。私はこの国で、江戸時代から継がれてきた技法を身につけた、現存する数少ない職人の一人です。今、私のような人間が行動しないと、日本の職人文化は間違いなく失われ、真の伝統工芸は残らなくなってしまいます。

　2021年6月、私はNPO法人「ROLE」を立ち上げました。漆芸師、指物師、表具師といった様々な役割（ROLE）を持つ職人たちがつくり上げてきた日本文化の復活と継承の想いを込めて命名しました。また、「ROLE」とは「Revival Of Lacquer Experience」の略号でもあります。

　私は漆芸修復師ですので、「漆で未来を変えたい」といつも思っています。私を含む職人の想いと行動に賛同する仲間が少しずつ増えて、伝統工芸が未来に繋がるきっかけになるのであれば、私はどんな「労」も惜しみません。その活動は、私にとって「労して苦せず」だからです。

Afterword

Work hard and suffer no pain

It is often said, "You must be willing to endure hardships while you are young." In fact, when I was in my teens and twenties, I had to go through a series of tough trials in order to assimilate the techniques from my master. But now, I finally understand why my master was so hard on me. My master had taught me that the skills one learns through one's own body are the very flesh and blood of a craftsman, the very essence of life. The experience of my apprenticeship has become an invaluable asset for me.

What I think now is that if something is important to me, I should be willing to do the necessary "labor" even free of charge. If it can provide my sustenance, even if it is hard "labor," it is not "hardship." On the other hand, if I receive good remuneration for a job that requires me to sell off my skills and time, then it is nothing but "hardship" and I will on principle refuse such requests.

Now, I have a big goal in mind. I want as many people as possible to understand the current state of Japan's traditional crafts, which are in decline, so that the skills required for those crafts can be passed on to future generations.

I am one of the few craftsmen alive today who have mastered the techniques that have been handed down since the Edo period. If people like me don't take any action now, Japan's craftsman culture will definitely be lost, and there will be no true traditional crafts left.

A few months ago, I launched a non-profit organization called "ROLE." The name "ROLE" was chosen to recognize the rich contribution made to Japanese culture by creative specialists such as lacquerware artists, sashimoto craftsmen, and paper frame mounters, and to express our hope that the culture which they created in their various roles would remain vigorous, and be passed on intact to future generations. The name "ROLE" is also an acronym for Revival Of Lacquer Experience.

Since I am a lacquer art restorer, I always want to change the future with lacquer.

I want the number of people who agree with the thoughts and actions of craftsmen such as myself to increase. If opportunities can arise for traditional crafts to be better understood and connected to the future, I will spare no effort to make it happen, because for me, such activities are certainly hard work, but not suffering.

謝辞

　本書に掲載した写真に関して、写真家の小笠原敏孝氏、加藤昭夫氏に大変お世話になりました。

　第1章の「漆兄弟と龍の淵」の挿絵を山本宗平画伯にお願いしましたところ、物語を彩るすばらしい絵を描いてくださいました。叡昌山本法寺の瀬川日照貫首には本法寺汲み出し茶碗修復をご用命いただき、その後の対談も快くお引き受けくださいました。琵琶法師の関川鶴祐師は、たくさんのお話を聞かせてくださいましたし、友人であるチェリストのウイリアム・プリンクル氏は演奏活動で忙しい中、拙著の英訳を進んで引き受けてくれました。高野教会には写真撮影の許可をいただき、私が修復した思い出深いマリア像を本書に収めることができました。一般社団法人大子町特産品流通公社には、これまでもたくさんの資料をご提供いただきましたが、今回も漆掻きの様子を収めた多くの貴重な写真をご提供いただきました。

　また、本書の企画、編集から刊行に至るまで淡交社編集局の江川真由氏には大層ご尽力いただきました。この場をお借りして、心より御礼を申し上げます。

　この機会に、私の手仕事を支えてくださるお取引先と職人の皆様に謝意を申し上げます。皆様の力なくしては、私の仕事は成立しません。

　そして、私の想いに共感していただき、サポートしてくださる映像作家の重森貝侖氏、お茶の水アートギャラリー884の佐野加代子氏とギャラリーに集う仲間の方たち、裏千家准教授の北島利津子氏、いつも力と元気を与えてくださる京都と東京の金継ぎ教室の生徒の皆様、私と共に歩む漆芸舎のスタッフに、心からの感謝を申し上げます。

　私は皆様と共に力を携えて、日本のみならず、消えつつある世界中の手作り文化の復活を願い、私の「日々一生」を歩んでまいります。

令和三年初秋
京都大徳寺前の工房にて

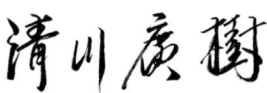

Acknowledgments

I am very grateful to the photographers Toshitaka Ogasawara and Akio Kato for their help with the photographs in this book.

I asked the artist Sohei Yamamoto to draw the illustrations for the first chapter, "The Lacquer Brothers and the Dragon's Pool," and he did a wonderful job of bringing the story to life. Nissho Segawa, abbot of Eishozan Honpoji Temple, entrusted me with the restoration of the tea bowl of Honpoji, and also graciously agreed to a conversation with me after the restoration was completed. The priest Kakuyu Sekikawa, also a famous biwa player, shared many stories with me, and my friend William Prunkl, a cellist, accepted to translate my book into English while he was busy performing. Takano Church graciously allowed me to take photographs of the statue of Mary which I restored, and to include them in this book.

I am grateful to Daigo Specialty Distribution Company (the General Incorporated Association) for providing me with many reference materials in the past, and this time also for providing me with many valuable photos of the lacquer scraping process.

I would like to express my gratitude to Mayu Egawa of the editorial office of Tankosha for her great efforts in the planning, editing, and publication of this book.

I would also like to sincerely thank filmmaker Bryon Shigemori, and Kayoko Sano, the owner of Ochanomizu Art Gallery 88, as well as her friends at the gallery, who share my passion and support my work. I also appreciate all the great support I receive from Ritsuko Kitajima, who is an Urasenke-school associate chado professor.

I would like to take this opportunity to express my heartfelt gratitude to all of my business partners and the craftsmen who support my handiwork. Without your help, my work would not be possible.

I would like to thank all the students of my kintsugi classes in Kyoto and Tokyo, who always give me strength and energy.

Finally, I'd like to express warm appreciation to the staff of my company, who work with me.

Together with all of you, I hope to maintain Japan's craftwork tradition into the future.

Early autumn of 2021
At my workshop in front of Daitokuji Temple in Kyoto

漆芸修復師

清川 廣樹

プロフィール

1957年4月大阪府生まれ。
幼少より絵を描くことが好きで美術大学を目指していたが、父親が早くに他界したため、高校卒業後、蒔絵師に弟子入りして職人としてのキャリアをスタートさせる。その後、文化財、神社仏閣、調度品などの修復の一線で活躍する複数の職人のもとで研鑽を積み、28歳で独立。45年間、江戸時代に確立された伝統技法の継承者として、漆を用いた「漆芸」修復に携わる。その対象は建築、仏像、陶磁器、漆器、アンティーク家具、古美術品など多岐にわたり、学術関係者との交流も持つ。
2015年春より、伝統工法を幅広く紹介することを目的に、京都と東京で金継ぎ教室を主宰し、自然素材のみで行う工法の丁寧な指導と、長年の職人生活で得た知識や様々な経験談を紹介。2017年より現在まで、日本橋三越本店で金継ぎ修復の見積り会を開催、イギリス公共放送BBC、テレビ東京等のメディア出演多数、雑誌、企業広報誌等で活動が広く紹介される。
また、文化サロンや講演などの仕事にも関り、京都FM87.0では月1回「金継ぎタイムトラベル」という冠番組を持つ。2014年5月、京都市北区の大徳寺東門前に工房をオープン、2019年7月に株式会社漆芸舎設立、代表に就任、2021年6月にNPO法人「ROLE」を設立し代表理事を務める。企業活動、NPO活動を通じて、後継者作りや文化保持に意欲的に取り組んでいる。

[TV]

イギリスBBC　Reel 2020年8月
TV東京　2020年10月19日放映「Youは何しに日本へ？」
　　　　2018年8月20日放映「世界!ニッポン行きたい人応援団」
　　　　2020年8月19日放映「ビデオレター」
その他、読売テレビ、テレビ朝日、フジテレビなどの各局に出演

[ラジオ]

KYOTO FM 87.0　2021年4月〜月1回

[雑誌・月刊誌・新聞]

京都新聞　2015年12月23日、2016年12月19日
朝日小学生新聞　2019年5月8日
淡交社「茶道具のつくろい」2019年10月
株式会社ウエッジ「ひととき」2019年2月
ぎょうせい「ガバナンス」2020年9月
日本橋三越「お帳場通信」2020年春夏号
野村証券「包 Wrap-i」2020年1月号　他多数

Lacquer Art Restorer

Hiroki Kiyokawa

Profile

Born in Osaka Prefecture in April 1957.

From a young age, he loved to draw pictures and wanted to become an artist, but his father passed away early, so after graduating from high school, he apprenticed himself to a maki-e artist and began his career as a craftsman. Later, he studied under several craftsmen who were active in the front line of restoration, becoming independent at the age of 28.

For 45 years, he has been involved in the restoration of lacquerware as an inheritor of the traditional techniques established in the Edo period. His work covers restoration of temples and shrines, architecture, Buddhist statues, ceramics, lacquer ware, antique furniture, and antiques, and he is highly trusted by academics. Since the spring of 2015, he has held kintsugi classes in Kyoto and Tokyo with the aim of introducing the traditional methods to a wide range of people. From 2017 to the present, he has held estimate sessions for kintsugi restoration at the Mitsukoshi Department Store in Nihonbashi, Tokyo, and has appeared in many major media outlets such as the BBC and TV Tokyo. In recent years, he has also been involved in cultural salons and lectures, and has a monthly program called "Kintsugi Time Travel" on Kyoto FM 87.0. He opened his current studio in front of the east gate of Daitokuji Temple in the north of Kyoto in May 2014, established Kiyokawa Lacquer Art Co. in July 2019, and established the NPO "ROLE," of which he serves as representative director, in June 2021. Through his business company and NPO activities, he is actively involved in creating successors and preserving traditional culture.

[TV]

BBC   BBC Reel "The Japanese art of fixing broken pottery," which premiered August 2020
TV Tokyo   "Why did you come to Japan?" broadcast on 19 October 2020
TV Tokyo   Special program broadcast on 8 August 2018, in which an Italian lady is invited to Kyoto to learn kintsugi.
TV Tokyo   Subsequent conversation with the Italian lady, in a video letter from Milan broadcast on 19 August 2020
Other appearances on Yomiuri TV, TV Asahi, Fuji TV, and other stations.

[Radio]

KYOTO FM 87.0 once a month from April 2021

[Magazines, monthly magazines, newspapers]

Kyoto Shimbun (daily newspaper): 23 December 2015, 19 December 2016
Asahi Shogakusei Shimbun (newspaper for primary schoolers): 8 May 2019
Tanko (monthly magazine) 2019 special issue, "Mending Tea Implements": Tankosha, October 2019
Hitotoki (monthly magazine): Wedge Corporation, February 2019 issue
Ochoba tsushin (Nihonbashi Mitsukoshi Department Store newsletter for VIP card holders): Spring/Summer 2020 issue
Governance (monthly periodical): Gyosei Corporation, September 2020
Ho, Wrap-i (newsletter): Nomura Securities, January 2020
and many others

継(つなぐ) 金継ぎの美と心
The Spirituality of Kintsugi

令和3年11月24日 初版発行

著　者	清川廣樹
発行者	納屋嘉人
発行所	株式会社　淡交社
本　社	〒603-8588 京都市北区堀川通鞍馬口上ル
	［営業］Tel. 075-432-5156
	［編集］Tel. 075-432-5161
支　社	〒162-0061 東京都新宿区市谷柳町39-1
	［営業］Tel. 03-5269-7941
	［編集］Tel. 03-5269-1691
	www.tankosha.co.jp

印刷・製本　NISSHA株式会社

©2021 清川廣樹　Printed in Japan
ISBN978-4-473-04485-3

定価はカバーに表示してあります。
落丁・乱丁本がございましたら、小社営業局宛にお送りください。送料小社負担にてお取り替えいたします。
本書のスキャン、デジタル化等の無断複写は、著作権法上での例外を除き禁じられています。また、本書を代行業者等の第三者に依頼してスキャンやデジタル化することは、いかなる場合も著作権法違反となります。

主要参考文献

内藤誠吾
教材研究「千年の釘にいどむ」『国語5年 上』
光村教育図書　2005年

小松大秀　加藤寛
『漆芸品の鑑賞基礎知識』　至文堂　1997年

松田権六
『うるしの話』　岩波書店　1964年

山久漆工株式会社	yamakyu-urushi.co.jp
中川政七商店	nakagawa-masashichi.jp
岩多箸店	wajimahashi.com
うるしの國・浄法寺	urushi-joboji.com
一般財団法人　古田織部美術館	furutaoribe-museum.com
戦国武将の名言から学ぶビジネスマンの生き方	kenplanning.sakura.ne.jp/www/

デザイン	久都間ひろみ［くつま舎］
写真	小笠原敏孝
	加藤昭夫
	大道雪代
挿画	山本宗平

Design	Hiromi Kutsuma　[Kutsumasha]
Photos	Toshitaka Ogasawara
	Akio Kato
	Yukiyo Daido
Illustration	Sohei Yamamoto

Tsunagu Kintsugi no bi to kokoro
The Spirituality of Kintsugi

By Hiroki Kiyokawa

This book was published in 2021
by Tankosha Publishing Co., Ltd.